How To Use
Plastic Sextants

With Applications to Metal Sextants and
a Review of Sextant Piloting

STARPATH®
Seattle, WA

Published by Starpath Publications
www.starpathpublications.com

3050 NW 63rd Street, Seattle, WA 98107

"Starpath" is a registered trademark of Starpath Corporation

Illustrations and book design by Tobias Burch

For contact with the author and news related to this book
see www.starpath.com/sextants

Contents

Acknowledgements

Most of the basic matters of sextant use have been known for two hundred years. In fact, it has been known so long, that much of it has been forgotten. The best references on the use of sextants are usually the very old ones. In light of that, we have the Google Books project to thank for ready access to many of these classic texts. (The jury is still out on the implications of this service for modern books. All matters of reading, writing, and publishing are in a state of flux these days. We have to wait and see.)

With these known matters in hand, however, we still had to learn the practical application of these skills ourselves. And to this end, I have been very fortunate to work with the best navigators and navigation teachers one could hope for. Larry Brandt, Steve Miller, Robert Reader, and Hewitt Schlereth have all made important contributions to presentation included here.

Robert has helped shape our teaching materials and helped with analysis since the first edition of this work, 10 years ago. Hewitt has been an expert on plastic sextants for many years before we started on this project, and his recent data at sea referenced here is just more testimony to his skill. Steve Miller has also used plastic sextants in his teaching for many years, and I am especially grateful for his extensive work on mastering their use for lunar distance measurements. A few are included here. To our knowledge, Steve is the first person to adapt the Baader Solar Films to sextant telescopes. We are grateful to Bruce Stark for suggesting we extend our plastic sextant work to lunars. It was a crucial step to making other improvements in the procedures.

A special note of thanks goes to Larry Brandt. Beside his great skill as navigator and teacher are his great skills as writer and editor. His sharp eye for detail and clear expression has saved the reader many a puzzling moment.

And finally, I am once again pleased to thank Tobias Burch of Starpath Publications for his production of the book, including all of the graphics and design. There has not been a graphic we have made for any book that he has not improved conceptually in the process of rendering it. His editorial suggestions on the text are always beneficial.

Preface

This small book started out as an even smaller booklet on plastic sextants alone. It concentrated on the nuances of plastic sextants and procedures we can use to overcome their inherent limitations in accuracy. It became clear fairly quickly, however, that the methods we are forced to use in plastic sextants to obtain practicable results are the same methods we could use to enhance our accuracy with metal sextants. So after continually directing our readers and students of metal sextants to the "Plastic Sextants Book" for optimizing their sights, we simply expand the name of the book and carry on—now somewhat less incongruously.

The focus is still on plastic sextants, because they present the biggest challenges. If you master their use, you will be even better with a metal sextant in your hand. It will always be obvious how to adapt ideas and procedures described for plastic sextants to the use of metal ones.

To broaden the topic to all sextants, we have adopted parts of our celestial navigation text directly related to sextants and sight taking, and included them here as well. But this book is not intended to teach celestial navigation. We assume the reader is already knowledgeable in celestial navigation or in the process of learning it from other sources.

We have also fine-tuned some of our plastic sextant use recommendations from earlier writing with the intention of pressing their use to even higher standards. The results are encouraging.

For plastic or metal, we are concentrating on details. If you want to do your best, the answers are all in the details. On the other hand, if you want to get started right away, here are the key points: treat plastic sextants as if they cost more than metal sextants do, and handle them gently, during and after the sights. Skim though Part 1 and read the section in Part 2 on Taking Sights, then start taking sights. Be sure to record all aspects of your sight taking sessions. The more sights you take, the more you can appreciate the importance of the details. You will see your results improve as you incorporate them into your "standard procedures."

Background

A sextant is a hand-held optical instrument used to measure angles between celestial bodies seen on the horizon or relative to the horizon. Its ingenuity lies primarily in its ability to measure these angles accurately, more or less independent of the motion of the person making the measurements. This is not a surprise, because it was invented for use at sea (in the mid 1700s), where the observer is moving about in the waves when sighting the stars. At sea or on land (with some form of artificial horizon) an observer can measure the angular heights of celestial bodies above the horizon to find their latitude and longitude on earth by means of *celestial navigation*. Measuring such an angle with a sextant is called "taking a sight."

Sextants can also be used to measure angles between terrestrial bodies to find the observer's position on a chart or map. This application is called *sextant piloting*. Explorers such as Lewis and Clark used both sextant applications in their famous expedition across the country, as did most of the early explorers on land and sea.

The forerunners of modern sextants were constructed of ebony wood with engraved ivory inlays for the dials. These were replaced with metal frames and gears. Measurement precision was enhanced by the invention of the vernier scale, which was then replaced in more modern times with a micrometer dial for easier reading.

Plastic sextants became available sometime around World War II for use in lifeboat navigation. Plastic instruments based on these early models were available to the public by the early 1960s, notably from Davis Instruments in the US and from East Berks Boat Company in the UK.

There is much anecdotal information about plastic sextants in magazines and online discussions, but progress with use of the instruments will go faster with a ready access to documented results, and to that end we have added throughout the text examples with all the details, with even more data in the appendix.

"The devil is in the details" is an excellent description of the plastic sextant. Without appreciating the care that must be taken, one is more likely to try it, not get the results hoped for, and abandon it—or more likely, write something derogatory about it, then abandon it.

Plastic sextants are often disparaged for lack of inherent accuracy and vulnerability to the effects of the sun. But while it is true that they are not as accurate as metal sextants and they are indeed more sensitive to the sun than metal sextants are (thermal expansion coefficients of plastic are some 10 to 30 times higher than for metals), plastic sextants can with special care still be used quite successfully for practical navigation at sea, and they provide a less-expensive alternative for new navigators to get their feet wet with sights of their own.

In some regards, plastic sextants are easier to use than metal sextants for the actual sight taking because they are so light weight, but this ease of handling is counterbalanced by the extra care required in procedures and analysis. The task at hand here is to explain the issues and then propose a way to compensate for these limitations by presenting a systematic method for taking sights with plastic sextants.

The question of thermal effects of the sun on the instrument when not in use should not be a real issue, since we have no reason to leave them for extended periods in the sun, just as we would not leave a thousand-dollar metal sextant in the sun. Whether or not they might thermally change during a particular sight session in the bright sun is not clear, though certainly possible. We have some data that might be explained by that, but it is not at all conclusive. We will address this issue in the section on sight taking procedures. There is also a related discussion in the Appendix.

Parts of a Sextant

To understand the limitations and issues at hand we need to look briefly at how sextants work. Figures 1-2 and 1-3 show two plastic sextants with a discussion of their parts. The Mark 15 is a micrometer drum sextant; the Mark 3 is called a vernier sextant as it has no micrometer drum.

Micrometer drum sextants have a series of notches cut precisely 1° apart into the outside

Sextant Parts in Fig 1-2 and 1-3	
A	Frame
B	Index arm
C	Index mirror
D	Index shades
E	Arc
F	Horizon mirror
G	Horizon shades
H	Telescope
J	Sighting tube
K	Clamp

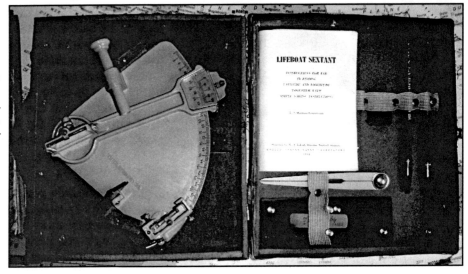

Figure 1-1. *This sample of the original US Navy lifeboat sextant (Culver 1940) is part of the collection of Francois Meyrier, sailor, celestial navigation instructor, and author. It is slightly larger and of heavier plastic than its grandchild, the Davis Mark 3.*

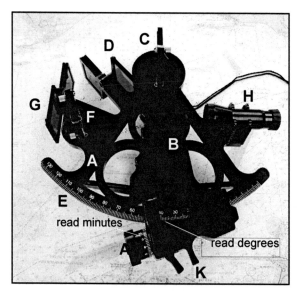

Figure 1-2 *A Davis Mark 15 sextant. It has a 7" frame radius, with a 3 x 27 telescope (magnification of 3, diameter of lens 27mm). The arc reads from -5° to 120°.*

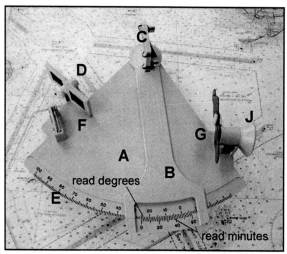

Figure 1-3. *A Davis Mark 3 sextant. First models date from about 1963. There is "sighting tube" in place of a telescope.*

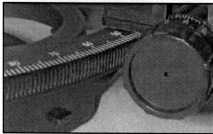

Figure 1-4 Top *Close up of the worm gear on a metal sextant. A similar mechanism is encased in plastic in the Mark 15. When the clamp is compressed it pulls the worm gear out of the notches in the arc.*

Figure 1-5 bottom *Close up of the arc and gear rack on a Mark 15.*

edge of the arc of the instrument. The notches are labeled in degrees along the side of the arc. A worm gear at the base of the index arm presses into these notches as it moves along the arc. This gear is encased in the plastic of the Mark 15. A similar design on a metal sextant is shown in Figure 1-4. Large changes in sextant angle are made by squeezing two levers that disengage the worm gear and allow the index arm to slide along the arc. Releasing the levers engages the worm gear once again, but sometimes a slight twist of the micrometer drum is needed to seat the gear properly. The degrees part of the new sextant angle is read from a reference mark on the index arm against the degrees scale printed or engraved into the side of the arc. Angle changes with the vernier model are made by sliding the index arm manually along the arc.

The Mark 15 comes in a functional plastic case. A "sighting tube", included in the case, is sometimes used with sextant piloting. There is also a string tied to the sextant which is intended as a neck strap, but this will certainly cause more trouble than good and should be removed. If a neck strap is called for then a large piece of soft webbing as used for sail ties would be better.

The eye piece of the telescope also comes with a small plastic cup. This cup, too, can be completely removed and not used, but if it is to be left on then it should be trimmed by a couple mm because it is slightly too long. As is, it can inhibit the telescope adjustment tube from being pushed all the way in, which in turn prevents getting the best focus from the telescope. As discussed later, we do not want to touch the scope to our forehead (or glasses) so there is no need for this cup.

The Ebbco sextant is an intermediate design style. It has a solid arc similar to the Davis Mark 3, but then includes a micrometer drum for the minutes, which is more similar to the Davis Mark 15. A sample is shown in Figure 1-6, along with another US Navy forerunner of plastic sextants in Figure 1-7. Ebbco sextants have been cherished by their users for many decades.

The Davis Mark 25 is essentially identical to the Mark 15, but is fitted with what is most often called a "full-view mirror," or "whole-horizon mirror," although neither is what Davis calls them, and Davis is the company that invented this alternative horizon mirror for sextants. It is now offered as an option by most sextant manufacturers. The original Davis patent for the design is available online.

There are pros and cons to the full-view mirrors; there is not a simple answer—again, the devil is in the details.

If you have never taken a sight before and are presented with a sun in midday with a dark blue sea and light blue sky, and you were asked to compare the two types of sextants, you would almost certainly choose the full-view style. It will at this first use of a sextant in these ideal conditions seem easier. And indeed it is this reaction that has led many new users to choose this option.

What you soon will learn, however, is that this is indeed a very easy sight, and regardless of what sextant you have in your hand, you will in a few minutes of practice be doing it just fine

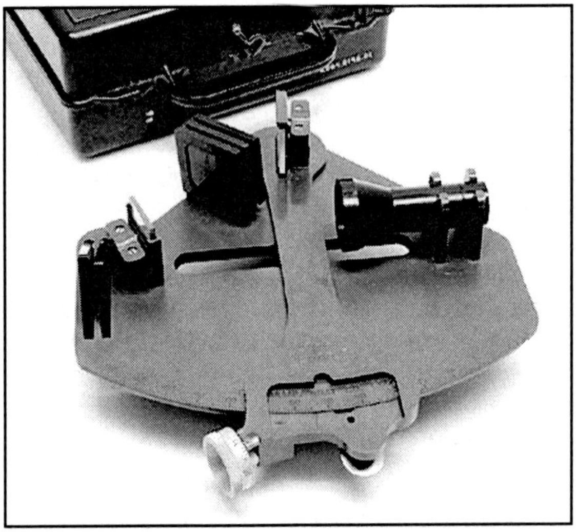

Figure 1-6. *An Ebbco sextant. Once available in the US, but now only in Europe. We have had one for 20 years, which still works well, but a couple of the shades have gone opaque with age. The telescope (2.5 x 28) is about the same as the one on a Mark 15. Further notes on the Ebbco are in the Appendix.*

Figure 1-7. *A US Navy grandparent of plastic sextants made by Felsenthal Plastic Company in Chicago, the origin of the 2102-D Star Finder. During WW II this company produced 90% of the Navy's plastic navigation tools. From the Smithsonian Museum, with bubble attachment for aircraft use.*

with a traditional horizon mirror, which is half silver and half glass. With this standard type of sextant horizon mirror (used since 1750's) you do have to coordinate keeping the sextant pointed toward the object as you move around some and rotate (rock) the instrument. With the full-view model, you have broader leeway here and this is easier. We cover details of the sight taking section of Part 2.

On the other hand, for other sights, things are completely different. The full-view mirror works by splitting the light spectrum in half according to color, by means of special optical coatings on the glass. This special surface reflects the bluish half and transmits the yellowish half, as shown in the Appendix. The net effect is you see at the same time light passing through it and light reflected from it—but only roughly half of the light intensity in each case. Hence the problem. For faint stars, you are losing half the light so the stars are more difficult to see.

But that is not the main problem. The main problem comes in when viewing anything that is about the same color as the sky. A daytime moon in a "white" sky, for example, can sometimes not be taken at all with that style of mirror. Also when the sea and sky are nearly the same color—which is fairly often—then it is very difficult with this model to check the index correction using the horizon.

Another drawback shows up when you use the sextant for coastal piloting, either with vertical sextant angles or horizontal angles, such as the famous three-body fix, which is such an accurate means of piloting it is usually called sextant surveying. In these sights you are looking at land overlapping land images where they often differ only in the shade of color. These sights are significantly more difficult with the full-view type of mirror.

In a nutshell, "full-view" mirrors make the easy sights easier and the hard sights harder. We generally do not recommend them unless the primary intended function is sun sights at sea as a back-up to electronic navigation. If you will be using the sextant for its full range of functions, the traditional mirror is a better choice. On the other hand, Davis sells the mirrors separately, so one could in principle replace the full view mirror on a Mark 25 with a traditional mirror from a Mark 15. Such a change, however, would be more or less permanent. It is not feasible to change them at will for different applications. The change is easy, but tedious, because the clamping springs are very tight.

For completeness we should mention this exception. Very high sights (angles above some 85°) are difficult because with the sun essentially overhead it is difficult to keep the sextant pointed toward the sun's direction—it is very

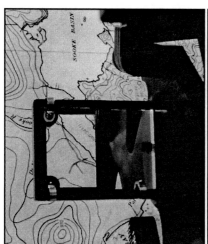 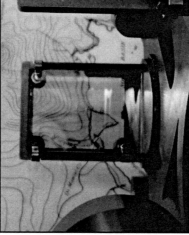

Figure 1-8. *Horizon mirror options. Left is the traditional half-split mirror used on a Mark 15, with clear glass on the left side and mirror on the right side, here reflecting another part of the sextant. On the right is a Davis Mark 25 "full-view" mirror that has the same optical coating over the full horizon glass. Davis called the coating a "beam converger," but the name never caught on, and even Davis now describes it as "full horizon." More details are presented in the Appendix.*

figuratively like deciding which way is south at the North Pole. These high sights are definitely doable, but it takes special techniques in both the sight taking and of course in the analysis. You cannot use conventional sight reduction methods for near-overhead sights. For these rare sights, a full-view type of mirror makes them a bit easier than a split-view mirror. That said, we still do not change our recommendation.

Full view and traditional horizon mirrors are shown in Figure 1-8.

Sextant Principles

A sextant measures the angle between two objects using a double reflection principle shown in Figure 1-9. To measure the height of a star above the horizon, we look at a light ray from the star in the horizon mirror after it has been reflected from the index mirror alongside a direct view of the horizon through the horizon glass. The measurement is made by moving the index arm until the star is precisely even with the sea horizon.

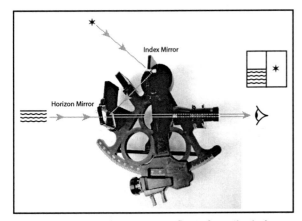

Figure 1-9. *Light from a star reflects from the index mirror, then from the mirror side of the horizon mirror, and then into the telescope. The horizon can be viewed directly through the clear-glass side of the horizon mirror. The angle of the star above the horizon is read from the arc when the reflected image of the star aligns with the direct view of the horizon, as shown in the insert.*

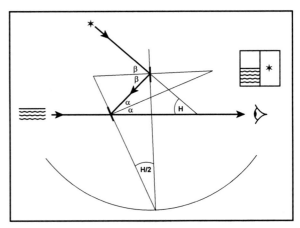

Figure 1-10. *When light reflects from a mirror, the angle of reflection equals the angle of incidence, from which geometry can prove that the height of the star above the horizon (H) is equal to twice the angle between the mirrors. This way a sextant with a frame arc of one-sixth of a circle (60°) can be used to measure angles of up to 120°.*

Though at first it might not be apparent, the index arm of the sextant only moves half as much as the angle being measured, as shown in Figure 1-10. For those who like such things, it is a nice geometry exercise to prove this.

The angular height read from the arc and micrometer drum presumes that the two mirrors are precisely parallel to each other when the dial

Figure 1-11. *The index correction is how much the two mirrors differ from exactly parallel when the dial is set to 0° 0'. There are several ways to measure this.*

reads 0° 0'.0' as shown in Figure 1-11. If they are not parallel, the instrument has an Index Error, and this must be accounted for with an Index Correction. Procedures for measuring and adjusting the index correction are covered later.

Side Error Adjustment

Another adjustment that is crucial for accurate work in both sight taking and in measuring the index correction is aligning the two mirrors to be precisely perpendicular to the frame of the sextant. When the mirrors are not perpendicular to the frame, the instrument is said to have a *side error*.

The adjustment proceeds in two steps, first adjust the index mirror using a view of the arc as shown in Figure 1-12. You can do this with the arc alone (without the dice), but it is easier and more accurate with something like the casino dice shown. Used casino dice (3/4 inch cube) are just a dollar or so online or at a casino and perfect for the job.

Once the index mirror is plumb, we need to go outside to view a distant landmark or horizon to make the horizon mirror parallel to the index mirror. One easy way is to view a star. Set the index arm to 0° 0' and view a star through the telescope, and adjust the telescope tube for optimum focus, as discussed in Figure 1-13. You will most likely see two stars, one in the direct

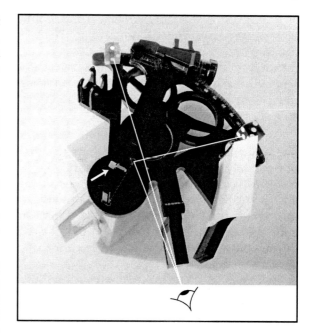

Mirror leaning forward

Mirror perpendicular

Figure 1-12. *Procedure for setting the index mirror perpendicular to the sextant frame. Top shows the setup. Place a dice cube at each end, then move the index arm till you can see both as shown below. We have put a Post-it over the horizon mirror to stress that it does not enter the process. We are viewing reflections from index mirror alone. It can be easier to remove the telescope, but if so, do it carefully (see Fig 1-13). Elevate the sextant on a table so you can sight the dice parallel to the arc and adjust the indicated screw until the dice tops are level. Then gently flick the mirror housing to be sure the mirror and springs are set, and double check the alignment. When this is right, the reveal of the mirror usually will be symmetric on all sides. If this is not the case, try setting it so ahead of time and start again.*

view and one in the reflected view. They should be relatively close, but will not overlap. The vertical separation between the two is the index error, which we address later, and the horizontal separation is a result of the side error, meaning the lack of parallelism between index and horizon mirrors. See Figure 1-14.

The next step is to adjust the tilt of the index horizon mirror to move the two stars together horizontally. This is done with the horizon mirror screw that is farthest from the plane of the arc. Laying flat, it is the top one, but this adjustment must be done as you hold the sextant to your eye viewing the star, so it will then be the outside one, on the left, which is the easiest one to reach.

The challenge, however, is that at this stage the index error and side error are interrelated to some extent. When you turn the adjustment

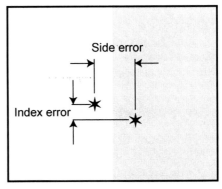

Figure 1-14. *Looking toward a star or planet with the arc set to 0° 0' showing side error and index error.*

screw to tilt the top of the mirror toward or away from the telescope to adjust its perpendicularity, you will also shift the side of the mirror somewhat, which will change the index error.

So it is an iterative process. Remove the side error, then use the other screw on the horizon mirror to remove the index error. This is the screw that is difficult to reach without blocking your view of the star. You must reach up and over the view to the star.

Then go back and forth as needed to get them both as small as possible. Try tapping or flicking the mirror housing periodically to insure the mirror and springs are set properly. (Don't flick it any harder than you would flick your own nose!) These errors do not need to be totally removed by adjustment, however, because we must in any event measure the residual index correction very carefully, as explained in a later section. It is valuable, however, to remove the side error as best you can at this stage.

Figure 1-13. *The telescopes on the Mark 15 and Mark 25 are identical (but for color). The front lens is 27 mm in diameter and the power of the scope is nominally 3x. The main body of the scope can be carefully slid out of the holding brackets as needed. These brackets are fragile, but if one breaks you can hold the scope in place with a post office rubber band. The eyepiece tube slides in and out of the main tube for focusing. The tolerances are just off on some units and it might help to file off the main tube a mm to allow for better distance focusing. Likewise the eyepiece cup can prevent the tube from moving in far enough, so trimming it a mm or so can help—or leave it off completely as it is not needed. If the fit is so tight that pressure pushes the tube back out, then drill a small hole in the large tube to prevent that.*

This can also be done with the sun (Figure 1-15) or the moon (Figure 1-16). With the sun, and sometimes the moon, you will see the reflected image of the sun on the horizon glass as well. This is just the sunlight reflecting from the surface of the horizon glass. It is a gift that makes the sun and bright moon measurements easier. It does not work for the stars, but might for a bright planet. Thus if you get stuck one day

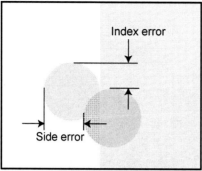

Figure 1-15. *Looking toward the sun with the arc set to 0° 0' showing side error and index error.* **CAUTION:** *you must use proper filters on both the horizon and index mirrors when doing this. See Index Correction section for a good custom filter solution and important safety discussion. This is dangerous when done wrong. If in doubt, use a star or a landmark.*

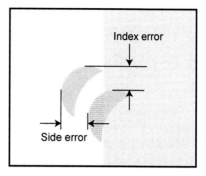

Figure 1-17. *Looking toward the moon with the arc set to 0° 0' showing side error and index error. Sometimes you must rotate the sextant to see the moon orientation properly in the mirrors, especially when measuring the index correction. For zeroing both errors as a starting point, this is not so crucial.*

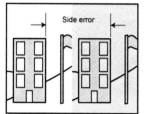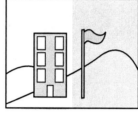

Figure 1-16. *Using a distant vertical landmark to gauge and remove the side error. The left is with mirrors not plumb; the right is corrected. At sea during daylight hours you can turn the sextant sideways and use the horizon as your "vertical" line.*

without any horizon mirror, even a plain piece of glass will serve as a "whole-horizon" mirror for sun sights.

The side error can also be adjusted using a distant tower or building edge, at least a couple miles away. Or even the sloping side of a distant hill can be used. At sea you can turn the sextant sideways and actually use the horizon for this side error adjustment. The moon can also be used, and in the index correction section we also discuss using special filters to use the sun, but a star or planet is an easy way to get it set about right.

We have found that painting the screws with fingernail polish once adjusted has helped preserve the alignment of the mirrors, but we do not have enough evidence to suggest this might universally work. It is something to try. We have had very good luck with fingernail polish on a Mark 3, but it has a different arrangement of the adjustment screws. All is done with two screws on the index mirror.

We have spent a lot of time on the side error removal even though it does not really enter into the actual sighting error in many cases. In the end, it is the correction for the index error that is most crucial to accurate results. However, later we look at ways to accurately measure the index correction and these methods require that the side error be gone, or nearly gone, for best results. We will come back to the topic in the section on Index Correction. At this stage, just set them both as near zero as possible.

Reading the Dials

Before we get into taking sextant sights of various kinds, we take a look at how to read the dials once the angle has been set.

On a micrometer drum sextant, angle settings between whole degrees are made by rotating the micrometer drum. This rotation changes the angle continuously from one degree to the next. The drum settings can typically be read to a precision of 0.1' of arc making use of a vernier scale printed along the edge of the drum. Hence if a sextant were set to an angle of 32° 21.8', we would read the 32° from the scale on the arc, the 21' from the micrometer drum, and the 0.8' from the vernier scale.

On a Mark 3 vernier sextant, the degrees part is read from the arc and all of the minutes part is read from the vernier. They are nominally precise to 2', but you can estimate 1' readings with care. Good lighting and a magnifying glass are often helpful, especially for the vernier dial reading, which requires careful judgment of alignment.

Below are instructions on reading the dials of a sextant and discussion of the nuances that might arise.

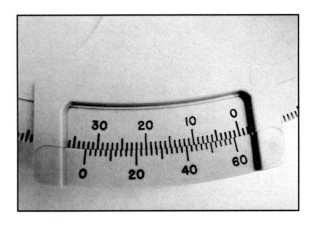

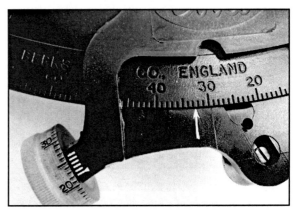

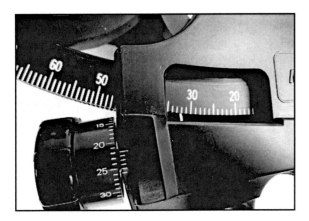

Figure 1-18. *Micrometer drum and vernier scale reading 32° 21.8' on a Mark 15 (left) and Ebbco (middle right) plastic sextants, and also on a metal sextant (bottom right). The Davis Mark 3 (top right) reads 32° 22' which is the closest it can be read—periodically the vernier alignment will be equally off on two numbers and then we can estimate an odd arc minute reading, as discussed on the following pages.*

Step 1

Notice that the index marks align exactly with the numbers. The degrees increase when you move the index arm to the left, out away from you. The minutes increase as you "unscrew" the micrometer drum, counterclockwise.

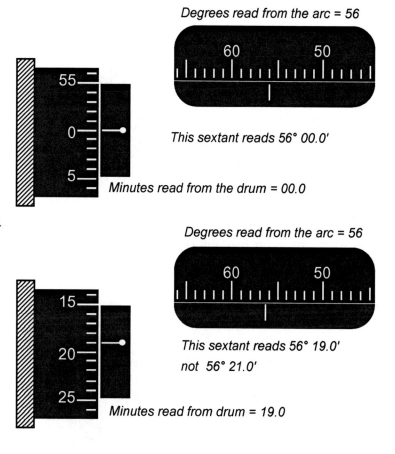

Degrees read from the arc = 56

This sextant reads 56° 00.0'

Minutes read from the drum = 00.0

Step 2

Notice that index mark on the arc is past the 56, about one third of the way to the 57. We can't tell that it is one third exactly, but we can tell that it is less than half. The minutes must be less than 30, as they are. The minutes align exactly with 19.0.

Caution: A possible mistake is to read the scales the wrong way and interpret this as 21'. Always check which direction is increasing before reading the dial. This type of error could be 2' (ie 19 vs 21) or as large as 8' (ie 16 vs 24). The smaller ones might be hard to detect later on.

Degrees read from the arc = 56

This sextant reads 56° 19.0'
not 56° 21.0'

Minutes read from drum = 19.0

Step 3

In cases like these, first check the minutes on the drum so you can interpret the degrees on the arc. After checking the direction, you see this is 58', or almost one full degree. So the degrees part of the angle must be just under 56, not just over it. Caution: Always double check your readings, especially when the degrees marker is almost exactly lined up. This type of error, however, is a large one that will usually be apparent in a series of sights of the same object.

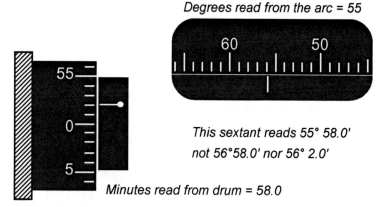

Degrees read from the arc = 55

This sextant reads 55° 58.0'
not 56°58.0' nor 56° 2.0'

Minutes read from drum = 58.0

Step 4

If the sextant looked like this after aligning the reflected and direct views of the horizon, the instrument would have no index error. During actual sights, always record that you have checked it, however, even if it was zero. We discuss measuring the index correction (IC) in the next section. For now we just focus on dial reading.

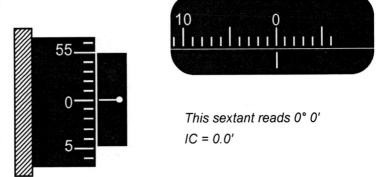

Degrees read from the arc = 0

This sextant reads 0° 0'

IC = 0.0'

Minutes read from the drum = 00.0

Step 5

Notice that the index mark on the arc is barely past the 0° mark. In many cases you cannot tell if it is to the left (on the scale) or to the right (off the scale). The drum reading, however, will always clarify this.

In this example, the index mark is halfway between the second and third mark, so the IC would be 2.5' on the scale. Notice, though, that without a vernier scale, we cannot really say if this is exactly 2.5. It could be 2.4 or 2.6.

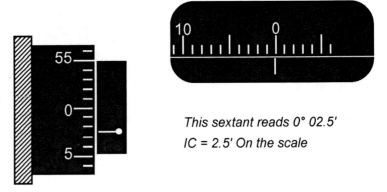

Degrees read from the arc = 0+

This sextant reads 0° 02.5'

IC = 2.5' On the scale

Minutes read from drum = 2.5

Step 6

For IC checks, you must nearly always tell from the minutes on the drum if you are off or on the scale. It will not be apparent on the arc for small corrections.

Be careful to count in the correct direction; this reads 58', not 2'. Alternatively, you can note it is off the scale, and then count the IC backwards. In this case, it reads 58 forward, which is the same as 2 backwards. With fractional readings (such as 58.7'), however, one must be careful with this, as covered later on.

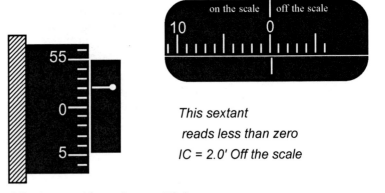

Degrees read from the arc = 0-

This sextant
reads less than zero

IC = 2.0' Off the scale

Minutes read from drum = 58.0

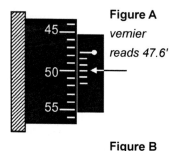

Figure A

vernier

reads 47.6'

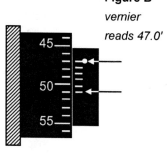

Figure B

vernier

reads 47.0'

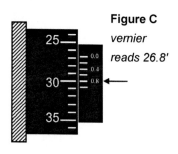

Figure C

vernier

reads 26.8'

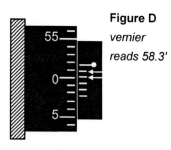

Figure D

vernier

reads 58.3'

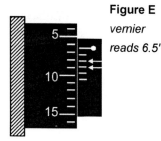

Figure E

vernier

reads 6.5'

How to read a vernier scale

Most sextants include a vernier scale next to the drum scale. This extra scale is used to interpret the proportional parts of the drum scale reading. If the index mark, for example, lies about halfway between 47' and 48' (as shown in Fig. A), it is the vernier reading that will tell us if this should be 47.4', 47.5', or 47.6'.

This clever arrangement of scales was an important invention from the early 1600's. Notice in Fig. B that the parallel scales are similar, except that the divisions on the vernier scale are smaller: five divisions on the vernier span only four divisions on the drum. The scale in Fig. B reads 47.0' because the index mark (or zero mark) of the vernier scale aligns exactly with the 47 on the drum. Notice, in this case, that the last mark on the vernier scale also aligns exactly with one of the drum marks (51 in this case). This is the way we tell that a drum reading is exact, the first and last vernier marks align precisely with two marks on the drum scale.

When the drum reading is not exact, the index mark of the vernier will not align with a drum mark, but one of the subsequent vernier marks will. The vernier mark that lines up is the one that tells us the tenths. Each vernier mark is 0.2' In Fig. A, the proper reading is 47.6', because the third vernier mark aligns with a drum mark. Notice that this third mark is the only one that lines up with a corresponding drum mark.

Some vernier scales are marked with numbers to help with the reading (as in C), but most are not. Scales with a dot or arrow marking the zero point and no other labeling are common. Our job, then, is to check the alignment, count the marks, and figure the tenths—then double check it.

Some verniers are marked in individual tenths (showing ten divisions instead of just five; quite nice, if you find one), but most are in two-tenth intervals. When the vernier is marked in two tenths, we have a problem with odd tenths. A 0.3 reading, for example, will not show a single exact alignment, but the 0.2 and 0.4 marks will be in closer alignment than any other, and these two will be equally unaligned in opposite directions, as shown in Fig. D. When there is no single mark aligned, look for two that are equally close. Always check the drum, however, to see that you are about right; that is, make a rough estimate from the drum reading alone, and then confirm the details with a vernier reading. If the drum and vernier read as shown in Fig. D during an index error check, the index error would be 60 - 58.3, or IC = 1.7' off the scale.

An example of a 0.5' reading is shown in Figure E.

Not all high quality (metal) sextants have verniers and in practice you won't really lose accuracy by estimating the tenths. Generally there are variations in individual sights that cause uncertainties and fluctuations in measurements of some 0.2' to 0.3', even with good instruments, in good conditions, and in experienced hands. Nevertheless, if you have a vernier scale, it is good procedure to use it.

We are being optimistic when using a vernier reading on a plastic sextant. These readings are not inherently that accurate, but in practice we will always do better to use the scale than not to. On the Mark 3 we must use the vernier as that is how we read the minutes themselves. We cannot even estimate tenths.

Index Correction Measurements

An ideal sextant has a very positive action of the micrometer drum, meaning no slack in the gears. Turn it to the right by 1' and immediately the angle increases by 1'. Stop, and turn it to the left, and it immediately starts to go down. A good metal sextant in good condition will behave properly in this regard. Plastic sextants, on the other hand, tend to have a bit of slack in this mechanism, consequently we get slightly different results when turning to the right to achieve alignment as opposed to turning to the left to achieve the same alignment. This is a well known issue with plastic sextants and it is mentioned in the manuals for the Davis Mark 15 and Mark 25 plastic sextants. It does not apply to the more basic Mark 3 model which does not have a micrometer drum.

But there is more to this story. We cannot investigate slack in the gears (of plastic or metal sextants) without some means of observing the effects of our rotation of the drum. In other words, we have to decide what is or is not in alignment once we rotate the drum. An obvious time to study this effect is during the index correction (IC) measurement, which is typically done with the sextant set to 0° 0.0' while viewing

a distant sea horizon. There are other, more accurate, means of measuring the IC, which might be applied to gear slack studies, but for now we discuss only the more common IC method of using the horizon.

The sea horizon is the most convenient and most commonly used method, but for precision work it has the limitation of not often presenting a perfectly sharp line between sky color and sea color. Look very carefully at the best horizon and you often see—or at least appear to see—a very narrow line of some other color right at the horizon, or some other slight disruption of a perfect line. Consequently, even when we have a perfect sextant with no gear slack at all, we can still get the appearance of a slight gear slack because the imprecision of the reference line leads to some variance from sight to sight in what the observer might call "perfectly aligned." The amount of this variance will depend on the nature of the horizon, the skill of the observer, the power of the telescope, and with the sextant model. For metal sextants, a 6- or 7-power scope is better for IC checks than the standard 4-power scopes, and this effect is naturally more of a challenge when viewed in the 2.5-power scopes on plastic sextants.

Investigating gear slack

First remove the side error of the sextant as explained earlier and then make this further check to see that it is removed: Viewing the horizon with the sextant set at 0°0' slowly roll the sextant about the telescope axis while carefully watching the horizon to see if you can detect any splitting of the horizon as shown in Figure 1-19. This rolling motion is called "rocking the sextant," discussed more in Part 2.

Removing side error may also require some collateral adjustment of the index mirror. As noted earlier, with plastic sextants we have found that it is often useful to give each mirror housing (not the mirror itself) a bit of a flick with the finger to help the seating of the mirrors before and after the adjustments. If the flick changes things, you have to keep working on it.

Then with the sextant set to 0° 0.0', view the horizon and turn the drum "toward" you (clockwise, angle decreasing) to clearly separate the two horizons viewed directly and by reflection. Then slowly turn the drum "away" from you (counterclockwise, angle increasing) until the horizons just first appear as a smooth straight line, which is what we call in alignment. Be sure to sneak up on this very slowly so you do not overshoot the alignment. We want the reading just as they first become aligned. Figure 1-20

Confirm that you are aligned by panning (yawing) the sextant right and left a bit to verify that there is no motion along the horizon. This is a more accurate method than just looking straight at it and concluding it is aligned. If you are just very slightly unaligned, you will notice a slight bump moving right and left at the intersection of the two views, direct and reflected, as illustrated in Figure 1-21.

Once confirmed, record the IC reading to the nearest 0.1' and label this IC measurement with an "A" to note that you were turning the drum in that direction and a "touch" to note that this was the setting for the first touch of the two horizon views in alignment. If you have overshot the alignment, start all over again.

Now to continue, first double check your notes to confirm which way you are turning and think through the motion, then very slowly and carefully continue turning in the Away direction until you can first detect that you are no longer aligned. Again, this is best done by doing a slight rotation then panning the horizon, then another and another pan, until you can detect some motion along the horizon which indicates that you are no longer aligned. Then read and record the new IC and label it with "A" and "leave," meaning this was the value when you left the alignment. See Figure 1-22.

Repeat this 5 or 6 times in the Away direction and then do the same in the Toward direction (turning the dial clockwise). This type of measurement will show what we are up against. You have effectively measured the angular width of

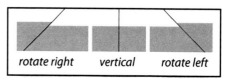

Figure 1-19. *Sextant with side error but no index error viewing the horizon and rocking the sextant. If there were also index error the vertical view would show a step at the mirror edge. If the horizon splits when you rock the sextant you need more work on the side error removal. When all side error is gone, the view will look like the middle one no matter how you rock the sextant.*

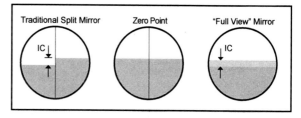

Figure 1-20. *Left and right are horizon views with the sextant set to 0° 0'. The middle is how it should look if there were no index error. The procedure is to set the sextant to 0° 0', view horizon then turn the micrometer drum till you see the middle view, then read the IC from the micrometer dial.*

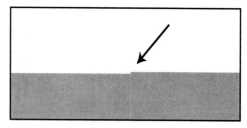

Figure 1-21. *When you think alignment has been achieved, yaw the sextant left and right a small amount to try to detect any little bumps moving along the horizon. This is often a more a sensitive way to confirm alignment, or lack there of, than just concentrating on the continuity of the line. As always, it is best to have all side error removed, because if you have a bit of side error and roll the sextant, the horizon will split even if it is perfectly aligned.*

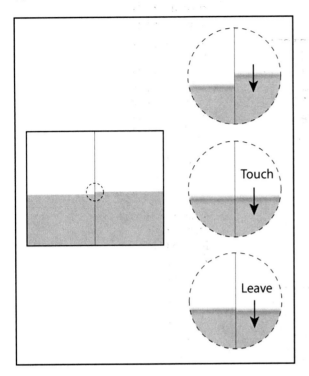

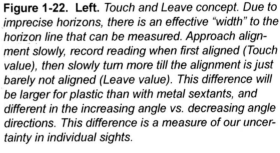

Figure 1-22. Left. *Touch and Leave concept. Due to imprecise horizons, there is an effective "width" to the horizon line that can be measured. Approach alignment slowly, record reading when first aligned (Touch value), then slowly turn more till the alignment is just barely not aligned (Leave value). This difference will be larger for plastic than with metal sextants, and different in the increasing angle vs. decreasing angle directions. This difference is a measure of our uncertainty in individual sights.*

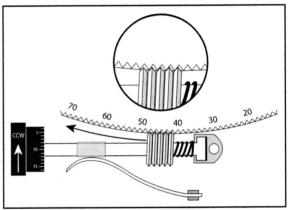

Figure 1-24. *Schematic of a Mark 15 worm gear mechanism. There are two crucial springs in the system. The flat one presses the gear against the rack, and the coiled one pushes the gear teeth against the teeth in the arc to compensate for slack in the gears, which is drawn exaggerated in the picture to show the contact side. When the micrometer is turned counterclockwise, the index arm with this mechanism attached to it moves to the left, increasing the sextant angle—the gear teeth remain in contact and under pressure throughout the movement.*

When the dial is turned clockwise to smaller sextant angles, the teeth momentarily disengage to push against the other side, and then when released the spring presses back on the original side. The spring takes out gear slack going either direction, but for decreasing sextant angle ("Toward") it does so in a more uncertain manner because it adjusts after you stop your turning. Thus it is best to make all final settings in the counterclockwise ("Away") direction.

Figure 1-23. *The backside of a Mark 15 with a cut out to show the worm gear and springs. The long flat spring holds the worm gear into the rack on the arc. Squeezing the clamps pushes the worm gear shaft down and disengages the gear to make larger angle adjustments. The coil spring on the left end is designed to reduce gear slack. The mechanism is discussed in Figure 1-24.*

For extensive details on corresponding parts and mechanisms on metal sextants, see W.J. Morris's excellent new book called The Nautical Sextant. *He states that even metal sextants will have a preferred alignment direction, which is usually in the increasing angle direction.*

"perfect alignment." With a metal sextant and a sharp horizon, the touch and leave values will typically differ by only a few tenths, which reflects our limits on locating the horizon precisely. Put another way, if we just randomly set the sextant to alignment on a series of sights, we could fairly expect to get at least this level of spread in the values we measured, since anywhere between "touch" and "leave" gives the same appearance of alignment.

More to the point at hand, however, is that with a metal sextant, the spread in the touch and leave values will show little if any difference when measured in the Toward or Away direction. With a typical plastic sextant this is not the case. Not only will you detect larger spreads in the touch and leave values, you will most often note a significant difference in the IC values measured in the Toward and Away directions, which is a measure of the slack in the gears—or, if not that, at least some measure of the general behavior of the device. The actual worm gear in the plastic sextants is metal, but it seats into the rack of notches in plastic, as shown in Figure 1-23.

Index correction differences in plastic sextants can also vary from day to day and from the beginning to the end of a given sight session—even if the temperature of the device has not changed significantly during the session. Sometimes the Toward and Away differences might be zero and other times on the same device (without having adjusted the mirrors) be as large as 4' or 5'. All final angle adjustments should be done in the Away direction.

I must admit that the use of "Toward" vs. "Away" for micrometer turning directions is not a tidy terminology for such an important concept, but it is not so simple to define as one might guess, because we turn the dials holding the instrument in different orientations. The table below shows some equivalent concepts. Our terms T and A evolved from the position of holding the sextant as you read the dials, but then when taking a sight, Away is to the right, and Toward is to the left. Just decide what works best for you, and then replace all of our Ts and As with your choice of notation.

We must stress here, however, that we are describing operational behavior and how to study it, and not necessarily a limit on the ultimate accuracy obtainable with the sextants. The exercise is intended to show how users might verify for themselves why special care must be taken when doing celestial sights with plastic sextants. Some metal sextant usage might also be improved by similar studies.

In the sight taking sections we show procedures that will to a large extent compensate for these limitations. Also, the IC is not always going to change indiscriminately on a plastic sextant. In the Appendix there is one testimonial from an instructor who had good luck with these as long as the temperature did not change. We have also had a Mark 3 with painted-shut adjustment screws that has shown stable mirror alignment over long periods of time.

Micrometer Turning Terminology*	
Toward (you)	Away (from you)
Not Correct for final adjustment	Correct for final adjustment
Right	Left
Clockwise	Counterclockwise
Screw in	Screw out
Decreasing sextant angle	Increasing sextant angle
Bodies rise in the mirror	Bodies descend in the mirror

* This is true for Davis Plastic sextants and most metal sextants. Exceptions are the Ebbco plastic sextant and some US Navy WW II sextants, which have "backward" micrometers, where cw motion increases the sextant angle. Usually the right direction to finish on is the increasing sextant angle.

IC from the horizon

Now that we know the procedures we can look at an actual case study. The sights were taken on Maui, in July. Start time was 1557 local, sitting in the sun on a hot day viewing a distant sea horizon.

The first measurements were just "set and read," no attention to "touch" or "leave," but I did record the direction of the turn. A large "twiddle" of the drum (about 3/4 to a full turn off of alignment) was made between each sight.

Toward	Away
0.4 on	0.4 on
3.0 off	1.0 on
2.0 off	0.6 on
3.5 off	0.0
0.8 off	1.8 on
2.2 off	0.0
2.4 off	0.4 on

At this point, I did a much bigger than before twiddle of drum (3° or 4°), up and down, then measured two more and got:

0.2 off	0.8 off
2.6 off	0.8 off

Averaging all data points in T and A, we get:

IC = 1.9' off, when turning "Toward,"
and
IC = 0.3' on, when turning "Away."

Next I did a few more being very careful to note the touch and leave alignments.

Toward		Away	
Touch	Leave	Touch	Leave
1.8 off	4.5 off	0.8 off	1.6 on
2.0 off	5.2 off	0.8 off	1.8 on
1.8 off	4.0 off	0.8 off	2.4 on
2.0 off	5.4 off	0.8 off	2.2 on

The sights ended at 1616. Total time in the process was about 19 minutes, which is recorded because it was very hot out that day. Note that the touch and leave approach has much minimized the spread in data points (see list of values under Touch or Leave), probably simply because one has to be very careful to catch the alignment.

We get these averages:

Toward touch = 1.9' off

Toward leave = 4.8' off

Away touch = 0.8' off

Away leave = 2.0' on.

Conclusions. Clearly there is a big difference between Touch and Leave values. So for best results we must do the sights in a consistent manner that matches how we measured the index correction, being very careful to note not only the direction of turn but the first alignment, and then use the Touch values for the IC in all cases. The Leave values are the most subjective and clearly the more anomalous of all the data. It seems that in my random Away sights listed above that I must have had more of a tendency to "overshoot" the alignment when turning in that direction.

For this sextant—or more to the point, for this set of sights—you could use IC = 0.8' Off when turning Away and on the touch mode. Or consider using IC = 1.4' ±0.6' Off if we are not careful with touch vs leave. In Part 2 on taking celestial navigation sights the process of alignment is incorporated into the actual sight process. One of the main things we have learned here is the level of uncertainty in IC that can result from horizon measurements.

Solar IC method

This method is more accurate than using the horizon, but we must say right up front that this is the one place where celestial navigation can be dangerous.

CAUTION!

The method involves looking at the sun, which is always dangerous, but we are doing it with a telescope, which is even more dangerous. Thus we must be aware of this and always use the proper solar filters and be careful that you do not peek around the corner of any filter for a direct view to the sun.

This is an old method, used routinely by those explorers who did most sights on land with an artificial horizon such as Lewis and Clark in the US and David Thompson in the US and Canada. The method was described by Nevil Maskelyne in his famous *Tables Requisite* as early as 1766.

It can be quite accurate, and offers a quick consistency check by measuring the sun's semi-diameter (SD) at the time of the sight, which can then be compared with the value listed in the Nautical Almanac.

It is not entirely clear, however, if this solar IC method is superior for routine sights at sea using a true sea horizon, since it is this sea horizon that we must use for a reference in taking the sights. In these cases, it could be that the conventional methods we discussed earlier might be preferred. My own sights at sea over the years were all done with horizon measurements of IC using a 7-power scope and mostly metal sextants, and I believe they generally fall within the best range of accuracy we can typically hope for, namely well below ±1 nmi. Whether or not they might be improved with solar IC data, I do not know. Generally correcting for the motion of the boat during sight sessions is the dominant factor on accuracy limits underway. However, I do not have much data other than that presented later here on plastic sextants at sea, and it is indeed likely that this solar IC method would be best for plastic sights in all conditions.

For lunar distance sights, on the other hand, the solar method is undoubtedly best. Landlocked, using an artificial horizon, this is the best method as well.

Solar IC procedure

With a metal sextant you would use the highest power scope you have for this, which would likely be a 6x35 or 7x30 monocular. With stock plastic sextants you have just the 2.5 power scope. Later we discuss ways to improvise to get higher powers.

Figure 1-25. *A Mark 15 with a homemade sun filter by Capt. Steve Miller, Dean of Education at Chapman School of Seamanship. This one uses the excellent foil from Baader AstroSolar Safety Film. The Appendix has instructions for making the filters that are intended to go over the front of the telescope. It is just a thin foil glued to the end of a short cardboard tube made to fit over the telescope as shown. No further shades are needed on Index or Horizon mirror for the solar IC measurements. A few wrinkles in the surface of the filter will not interfere with the measurements. His lunar sights with this instrument are included in Part 2.*

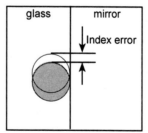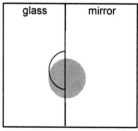

Figure 1-26. *Looking at the sun with sextant set to 0° 0', we see the vertical gap that is the IC we want to measure. The side error has been removed completely before starting. It is difficult to do this method if there is any side error. Remember you can see the reflected view on the glass side, but you cannot see the direct view on the mirror side. As you yaw and roll right and left slightly while looking at the sun it will switch between these two views.*

There are two approaches to the all important sun shades in this method. You can use the ones that come with the sextant, or you can make your own as described in the Appendix. A homemade one like the one shown in Figure 1-25 will generally work better than the stock shades for this job, but you can use the stock shades if that is all you have.

The Baader solar filter will leave both suns about the same color so we have to keep track of which is which, but with stock shades you can adjust the two sets of shades so the reflected and direct view of the sun appear as different colors. Then record the colors of direct and reflected images. A notebook and copious notes are a boon to progress with plastic sextants!

Start by setting the sextant to 0° 0.0′ and with the sun filters in place, look toward the sun on a clear day. You will see something like that shown in Figure 1-26, where we use the convention that shaded sun is the reflected view mainly on the right side of the horizon mirror but also some glass reflection on the left side as well, and the un-shaded one is the direct view through the clear glass of the left side of the horizon glass.

The vertical gap between the images is the index correction we want to measure. In an earlier method, we simply adjusted the micrometer drum till they overlapped and then read the IC from that dial. In this method we do it differently. We instead measure the angular height of the sun, top to bottom, then bottom to top. Then the difference between the two results divided by 2 is the IC. The mathematical principles of the method are explained in the Appendix.

For plastic sextants we must do this both for the Toward alignments and for the Away alignments, but you will find that this method is accurate enough to also detect differences using metal sextants. These latter differences could as much be part of the users personal bias as to what is aligned when going in one direction relative to the other, but if you do get consistent differences it is something to account for with any sextant when you want to do the best job possible.

First measure the "Toward" value of the IC using the sequence of steps shown in Figure 1-27. This starts with an Away rotation to separate the images. Then turn the micrometer Toward you slowly and uniformly so the reflected image rises till its top edge (called the upper limb) just touches the bottom edge (called lower limb) of the direct image (Step 7 in the picture). Then read the dial. It should read something like 32′ On the scale—depending on your IC. Record this ON value to the tenth of a minute in a simple form like that shown in Figure 1-28. In the example shown this was 34.0′ ON.

Now continue to turn, slowly and uniformly, in the Toward direction until the bottom edge of the reflected image aligns with the top edge of the direct image. If you overshoot, we need to start all over again! The idea is to be turning only in one direction when we stop. This time the dial will read about 28′ but this will be an OFF the scale measurement, so we have to subtract whatever it reads from 60. In this example, the micrometer read 29.2′, which would be 60.0′-29.2′ = 30.8′ OFF the scale. Record this OFF value as shown.

Now take the difference between the ON value and the OFF value and divide that by 2 to find your IC. Just subtract the smaller from the larger. The label of your result will be the same as the label of the larger value. In this example: 34.0 - 30.8 = 3.2′ and 3.2′/2 = 1.6′ and since 34 was ON, the answer is ON, ie our IC is 1.6′ ON the scale.

Now check your result by comparing to the actual semidiameter of the sun at the time of the sight. Our example was measured on 02/28/01 using an Astra 3b deluxe model sextant with traditional mirror. From the Nautical Almanac, we get that SD = 16.2′. The SD of the sun equals the ON value plus the OFF value divided by 4. In this example, 34.0+30.8 = 64.8 and 64.8/4 = 16.2 which is right, so we can have confidence that we have made good measurements. Several of examples from plastic sextants appear later in the book.

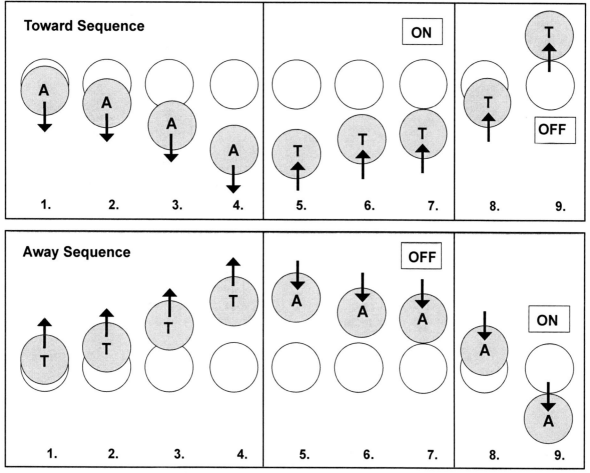

Figure 1-27. *Sequences for measuring the sun's semidiameter using Toward and Away rotations of the microm-eter drum. Toward is clockwise; Away is counterclockwise. Think of Away as the direction the top of the drum moves as you turn it ccw. If you overshoot on Step 7 or 8, you get to start all over again! Remember it is only the reflected image (shown here as a dark color) that moves as you turn the dial. The vertical location of the direct image in the horizon glass only changes when you alter the direction you are looking with the telescope.*

Also a reminder that the Toward sequence is only used when you are studying the gear slack effect. In actual sights you would use only the Away measurement.

Now you can repeat the full process turning always in the Away direction. Careful data will often show a slight difference for the Toward and Away values, even for a metal sextant. For plastic sextants, on the other hand, the toward and away values will almost always be rather large, some few minutes or so.

For what it is worth, after making these measurements, I usually make a quick look at the IC by horizon or by overlapping the sun or moon. The "solar method" will almost certainly be the right one to use, but this is just a check to learn what we might learn. If there is a significant difference in the methods, it might be worth pursuing, but you have to do the horizon or overlap methods very carefully before challenging the solar method results.

Date_____2/28/01_____SD_____16.2'_____   Date_____2/28/01_____SD_____16.2'_____

[Toward] or Away   Toward or [Away]

ON	OFF	Diff	Check SD
34.0	60.0	34.0	34.0
1.	− 29.2	− 30.8	+ 30.8
	= 30.8	= 3.2 ÷ 2	= 64.8 ÷ 4
		= 1.6 on	= 16.2

ON	OFF	Diff	CheckSD
33.6	60.0	33.6	33.6
1.	− 28.8	− 31.2	+ 31.2
	= 31.2	= 2.4 ÷ 2	= 64.8 ÷ 4
		= 1.2 on	= 16.2

ON	OFF	Diff	Check SD
33.8	60.0	33.8	33.8
2.	− 29.8	− 30.2	+ 30.2
	= 30.2	= 3.6 ÷ 2	= 64.0 ÷ 4
		= 1.8 on	= 16.0

ON	OFF	Diff	Check SD
33.4	60.0	33.4	33.4
2.	− 29.0	− 31.0	+31.0
	= 31.0	= 2.4 ÷ 2	= 64.4 ÷ 4
		= 1.2	= 16.1

ON	OFF	Diff	Check SD
33.8	60.0	33.8	33.8
3.	− 29.2	− 30.4	+ 30.4
	= 30.8	= 3.4 ÷ 2	= 64.2 ÷ 4
		= 1.7	= 16.05

ON	OFF	Diff	Check SD
33.4	60.0	33.4	33.4
3.	− 29.0	− 31.0	+ 31.0
	= 31.0	= 2.4 ÷ 2	= 64.4 ÷ 4
		=1.2	= 16.1

ON	OFF	Diff	Check SD
34.0	60.0	34.0	34.0
4.	− 29.6	− 30.4	+ 30.4
	= 30.4	= 3.6 ÷ 2	= 64.4 ÷ 4
		= 1.8	= 16.1

ON	OFF	Diff	Check SD
33.6	60.0	33.6	33.6
4.	− 29.2	− 30.8	+ 30.8
	= 30.8	= 2.8 ÷ 2	= 64.4 ÷ 4
		= 1.4	= 16.1

ON	OFF	Diff	Check SD
	60.0		
5.	−	−	+
	=	= ÷ 2	= ÷ 4
		=	=

ON	OFF	Diff	Check SD
33.6	60.0	33.6	33.6
5.	− 29.2	− 30.8	+ 30.8
	= 30.8	= 2.8 ÷ 2	= 64.4 ÷ 4
		= 1.4	= 6.1

ON	OFF	Diff	Check SD
	60.0		
6.	−	−	+
	=	= ÷ 2	= ÷ 4
		=	=

ON	OFF	Diff	Check SD
	60.0		
6.	−	−	+
	=	= ÷ 2	= ÷ 4
		=	=

average = (1.6+1.8+1.7+1.8) / 4 = 1.7' On   average = (1.2+1.2+1.2+1.4+1.4)/5 = 1.3' On
when turning in the Toward direction.   when turning in the Away direction.

Figure 1-28 *Work form for finding the IC by the solar method. This form design and data are from friend and navigator Lanny Petitjean using an Astra IIIb metal sextant with a traditional mirror. He has since used the results to achieve numerous sights from land with accuracies all below 0.4 miles and lunar distance sights leading to GMT accuracies below 30 seconds. The semidiameter (SD) of the sun or moon can be found in the* Nautical Almanac *or looked up online. T and A results are very similar, so more data would be needed to make conclusions.*

The virtue of the solar method is we are finding the IC by measuring a known value, the semidiameter of the sun, which can be looked up in the *Nautical Almanac*. Thus we have a consistency check of our results.

This method can also be applied to the Moon, which is often required when doing lunar distance measurements. This usually calls for some rotation of the sextant so you are moving the reflected image up and down parallel to the line drawn across the horns of the moon. Examples are given in the lunar distance section.

Caution on low-altitude solar method.

When the sun or moon is low in the sky (meaning below 15° or so, the solar method should be performed sideways, holding the sextant parallel to the horizon. This way you are using the "width" of the sun for the reference and not its "height." The problem with low altitudes is the refraction is changing so quickly with altitude that the apparent sun becomes squashed and we are not getting a true look at its SD with this method.

With the center of the sun 2° above the horizon (4 solar diameters), for example, the sun appears substantially above the horizon due to an illusion called the *moon illusion*, but it is still very low, where refraction is changing rapidly. At this elevation, the refraction at the top of the sun (Ha = 2° 16′) is 17.0′ and at the bottom of the sun (Ha=1° 44′) it is 19.4′. Thus we have an unaccounted-for uncertainty of some 2.4′ in a measurement we are striving to achieve with a few tenths of a minute accuracy. Using the width this uncertainty goes away, as it does for higher altitudes. At Ha = 15° the difference is less than 0.1′ and it gets even smaller going higher.

Differences Between Metal and Plastic IC Measurements

With metal sextants we often recommend an oversized eye cup for the telescope. They are available at camera shops. These have the advantage of blocking out all of the extraneous side light, which can help on faint sights, and they also give you another contact point for extra stability as you push your eye (forehead) against the soft eye cup. The small eye cups that come with many sextants do not do this job well. I have heard their purpose described as preventing eye glasses from clicking the scope, which may be a virtue on some level, but they do not serve for the task being described. The large cups work very well for metal sextants, but this trick will most likely not work at all with plastic sextants.

With plastic sextants we cannot press our eye against the sextant at all. If you push anything against any part of the instrument during a measurement it will distort the alignment—maybe move the target right out of view. To test this, line up the sun or a star on the horizon, and then very gently push on either mirror housing. The object will go right out of view. Likewise, even if you push on the telescope, it will shift the images on the level we are striving for, namely a minute of arc or so. With an Ebbco or Mark 3 sextant, if you squeeze the handle, the sun will move! Metal sextants do not behave this way.

So the message is we must handle them very gently when taking sights. No squeezing, no pushing, no touching the forehead. There is a time and place to tap the mirror housings as discussed earlier, but once you have done that and measured the IC, then nothing can be pressured from then on during the sights.

Another difference is in the procedures for setting the alignment. With metal sextants, we often teach that one way to set the alignment of body on body, or horizon on horizon doing the index correction is to turn the micrometer drum past alignment by some amount you can see and recall, then turn it back in the other direction by the same amount, and then repeat this process, as you gradually lower the amplitude of each swing. Then you end up on the alignment, in a sense coming from both directions.

You can also practice this with an assistant who reads your micrometer dial for you out loud as you turn back and forth with diminishing amplitudes. It is an instructive exercise, and this is indeed one way to do the IC measurement with a good metal sextant. It still pays to investigate the touch and leave characteristics of your sight taking as described, but then this might be the way you like to home in on the IC.

This method, which is quite nice for metal sextants, does not work for plastic sextants. It might even seem a logical way to do it with some slack in the gears, but it just seems to make things worse. You will quickly learn that almost all plastic sextants have a different IC in the Toward and Away directions, and this procedure just averages that out leaving you with half the accuracy you might have obtained.

Furthermore, there is a tendency in the Mark 15 and 25 to move in microscopic quantum steps as you turn the dial, rather than in a smooth advance. Sneaking up on an alignment in one direction alone makes this more evident, so you can be alert to this and then go back and start again with a setting if it jumps on you right at the last moment. The Ebbco does not show

this behavior as much, and the Mark 3 moves completely at your control, so this is not a factor with it.

With Mark 3 adjustments, we find the best adjustment is pressing the thumb against the arc next to the index arm and just slightly transferring some force to the arm in the lateral direction for a shift in angle. It is more of a gentle squeeze than a push that moves the index arm.

And of course the main difference between plastic and metal IC measurements is a good metal sextant will have an essentially permanent IC. Spend an adequate time studying it and you should be confident you know it to the nearest tenth of a minute. Then the job is just to do a quick check at the beginning of each sight session. But it does take time to learn it well. Remember the IC measurement is one part of routine cel nav that is typically underdone by new navigators, meaning many would get better final results if they spent more time on their IC measurements.

Sample Mark 15 Solar IC Measurement*								
	Date	SD	ON	60 -	OFF	IC	SD	dSD
A	8/2/2010	15.8	40.2	37.0	23.0	-8.6	15.8	0.0
A	8/2/2010	15.8	39.3	36.8	23.2	-8.1	15.6	-0.2
A	8/2/2010	15.8	40.0	37.8	22.2	-8.9	15.6	-0.3
A	8/2/2010	15.8	41.0	36.2	23.8	-8.6	16.2	0.4
					AVG=	-8.5	AVG=	0.0
T	8/2/2010	15.8	35.2	28.0	32.0	-1.6	16.8	1.0
T	8/2/2010	15.8	33.2	27.8	32.2	-0.5	16.4	0.6
T	8/2/2010	15.8	30.0	27.4	32.6	1.3	15.7	-0.2
T	8/2/2010	15.8	32.0	28.6	31.4	-0.3	15.9	0.0
					AVG=	-0.3	AVG=	0.4

SD is the sun's semidiameter. "60-" is what the micrometer read in the off-scale settings; subtract these values from 60 to get Off values. dSD is the difference between the measured SD (solar semidiameter) and the true SD. A negative IC here means it is ON the scale. "A" is turning away (ccw); "T" is turning Toward (cw).

It really does not matter how big the IC is, as long as you know it well. If it's more than a minute or two, it is likely best to adjust it back to below a minute. This you can do fairly easily. Then spend the rest of your time finding out what it really is. There is no virtue in having it be zero, because every time you tweak it trying to achieve zero, you have to start all over with the careful measurement process. So just set it by eye as close as you can and then measure it many times. If using the horizon, consider that a dark ocean against a light sky can give you a different result than a gray ocean against a gray sky, even with the traditional half-split horizon glass.

With plastic sextants we do not have the luxury of stable IC. It will change, and we just have to measure it and write it down. And unlike sight sessions with metal sextants, we should measure the IC before and after each round of sights. The IC measurement with plastic sextants is an integral part of the sight session; it is not just a check on something we already know.

With plastic sextants we are often setting the sextant IC before each session and then measuring it. Below is a sample solar method IC measurement for a Davis Mark 15 made today. The values are relatively large, and the Toward and Away are different, but using this data, we can get perfectly good cel nav sights from this instrument that is more than 20 years old.

The Toward and Away values differ by some 8', but both directions measured a relatively accurate semidiameter. In these particular measurements, the Away data (A) seemed smoother and easier to take, so one would be biased toward doing sights in that same direction—even though the actual IC came out much larger. This is, of course, the right choice, anyway, in light of past discussion here.

Figure 1-29 shows "sight tubes" that are sometime used to replace a telescope for sextant piloting applications. Figures 1-30 and 1-31 show two of the sextants we used in this study, which in a sense represent the opposite poles of the sextant world.

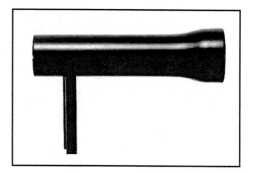

Figure 1-29 *Sight tubes sometimes called "collimation tubes" that replace the telescope in some piloting applications. They are not often an improvement over a telescope, but when no telescope is used it is valuable to have one to be sure the eye alignment is correct with the horizon mirror. Top left is a Mark 15, top right is a generic model with an attachment piece that fits most metal sextants from celestaire.com. Bottom left is the standard tube on a Mark 3, which is not an option, except in cases where the tube has been removed!*

Figure 1-30 *Our modified Mark 3. The sight tube has been cut off and the frame sanded flat. A Mark 15 telescope is attached with Velcro. We have sanded off a mm of the tube to insure full distance focusing and drilled a small hole in it to prevent pressure from pushing it back out (some are a tight fit). The mirror has been seated as best we can, then set to zero side error and IC, then adjustments painted tight with fingernail polish. (Double check both before painting!)*

A homemade Baader solar filter for IC measurements (Appendix) is stored in a pill jar. Also included is a small magnifying glass to read the vernier, which always takes much concentration for best reading. All is stored in a Rubbermaid #4 air tight container, lined with a stiff foam. Another piece of foam (under the box here) is used on top of the frame to hold all in place when closed.

The line on the frame reminds us to align the telescope and then check for a symmetric view of the horizon mirror before placing the sun filter on the front of the scope, because after that you can only see the sun. A detail of the scope rig is shown later in Figure 2-14.

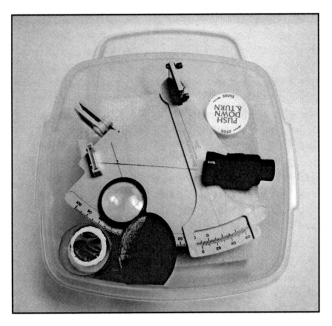

Figure 1-31. *A 1960 Toizaki sextant from Japan, No. 1016. It is our in-house example of a heavy sextant. At 4.6 lb, it is 12 times heavier than the mark 3 above. (The role of sextant weight is discussed in Part 2.) This one came with 7x35 monocular and a 10x inverting scope for doing horizon IC.*

The shades are both crossed polarized lens, which work well in most cases, but not all. The micrometer drum is marked in 10" intervals (0.17'), which turns out to be convenient and easy to read. 5" (0.08') is easy to interpolate. Also shown is a lens cloth for keeping the mirrors and telescopes clean, which is important for star sights.

Our homemade Baader filter is shown just sitting on the frame, out of its protective plastic jar. There is also a very dark eyepiece shade for solar IC using the monocular. The Baader filters always go on the objective (front end) of the telescope, not the eyepiece end.

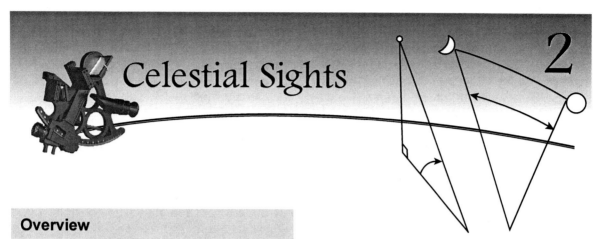

Celestial Sights

Overview

Celestial navigation is a way to find your position on earth from sextant measurements of the angular heights of celestial bodies above the sea horizon at known times. In a sense, the process dates to ancient Greek astronomy, but in practice the way we do it today can be dated to about the time of the US Civil War. For more background see Further Reading.

With a high quality metal sextant and good training in its use we can expect to obtain an accuracy in position of about ±0.5 nmi from a stationary vessel. Doing this from a moving vessel introduces other uncertainties that must be accounted for. Namely, if it takes me 30 minutes to complete a round of star sights, and I am travelling at 8 kts, then I must be careful when I say I know where I am to within ±0.5 nmi since I moved 4 miles during the measurement itself. Nevertheless, this is all doable, and standard texts (Further Reading) explain the procedures.

On the other hand, if we do not follow the best procedures, we might end up with uncertainties of, say ± 2 to 5 nmi, which I might venture is considered quite satisfactory results by many ocean cruising sailors.

In light of that estimate, we come back to what we might expect from plastic sextants. They will not be as good as the best metal ones in the hands of the same observers, but they will certainly do well enough for safe and efficient ocean navigation. This is in essence the main point of this book, and looking ahead we can say that this 2-to-5-nmi-accuracy is obtainable with the plastic sextants, but in this case using the best possible procedures is not an option. To get this good accuracy for celestial navigation sights from a plastic sextant we need to follow the guidelines listed here very carefully. Without following these procedures, then 10 to 15 nmi uncertainties would be more common.

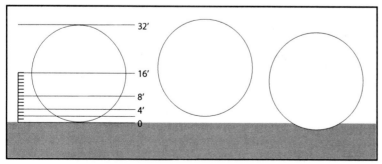

Figure 2-1 *The angular width of the sun from top to bottom is about 32'. If we misalign the sun with the horizon, our sights will be off about 1 nmi per 1' of error in this alignment. The middle sight would be off by 2 nmi in one direction, the right-hand side would be off 2 nmi in the other direction. If we end up with errors more than 2 nmi or so, then these are not likely due to alignment errors during the sights.*

Larger errors in plastic sextant data (when not done properly) are likely due to the Index Correction measurement and not accounting for backlash in the gears with a controlled measurement procedure. We know this must be the case, because the inherent alignment errors when taking the sights are much lower, as indicated in Figure 3-1.

Plastic versus metal

If you plan to go to sea for a long voyage and want reliable backup navigation, then a metal sextant is a good investment. A trip across the ocean could likely be navigated as well with a plastic sextant. Metal sextants are more accurate and easier to use in the sense that you mostly just pick them up and take the sights and put them away. They have much better optics, mirrors, and shades, so you can take the harder sights with good metal sextants much easier than with plastic. Plastic sextants, as we are learning, take special procedures, so the sight taking process is longer. On the other hand, the physical process of taking the sights is easier with a plastic sextant simply because it weighs less.

The lightest metal sextant weighs some three times more than a plastic one, so the plastic is much easier to handle, especially during a long sight session. Also, for coastal piloting, the plastic might even be preferred, which is consistent with its ease of handling.

Metal is much better from an investment point of view. Almost certainly the instrument you buy today will be worth more in a few years. This has been true for the past 30 years, and I see no reason that would change. The plastic ones, on the other hand—despite the fact that all prices go up each year—will have a resale value significantly less than its original cost. They simply do not hold their value, in part because of a false public awareness that they are not quality instruments. Maybe this book can help change that!

Brass versus aluminum

Just about any metal sextant that is not damaged will do the job and provide essentially the same level of accuracy in the final fix at sea. It is true that brass alloys can be machined to a higher precision in some cases, and as a result, you may see sextants with brass arcs quoting an accuracy of $\pm10''$ ($\pm0.17'$) compared to aluminium alloy arcs quoted as $\pm20''$ ($\pm0.33'$).

The reality, however, is we cannot rely on single sights for accurate results. The spread in errors of individual sights we must average will be of the same magnitude as these quoted uncertainties (at best), so there is no practical significance to the difference in accuracy for cel nav underway. If someone who has done 1,000 sights does another 100 with a good brass instrument and another 100 with a good alloy instrument, they will not be able to tell the difference in the results.

As far as final accuracy goes, it is far more important to use the right procedures and choose the right bodies to sight than it is to have a brass versus aluminium alloy. In fact, a main point of this book is if you do not use the right procedures, choose the right bodies, and analyze the results optimally, you might do as well with a plastic sextant as with a metal one!

Sextants do, however, vary in their ease of use. Key factors are the size of the mirrors, style of mirrors, kinds of telescopes, and weight. Weights vary from about 2.5 lbs for aluminium alloy models to over 4 lbs for brass models.

Role of sextant weight

As noted, light weight is a big advantage in sextants, because when the arms tire, we are not as careful as we should be when deciding alignment has been achieved. Do not be misled by advertising or other writing we might read that claims "professional navigators" prefer a heavy instrument, because it has inertia and is more stable. Sometimes the word "heft" is used.

The popularity of this line of thought can likely be traced to Lecky's *Wrinkles in Practical Navigation*. He starts off with a logical argument that a larger sextant can have a larger arc with better spacing of the angle marks, and thus it can be read more accurately. But instead of going on to say something like "but the price you pay for that is increased weight," he instead digs himself into a bit of a hole by stating that (a smaller sextant) "is of course somewhat lighter to handle, but sailors are not women; and a certain amount of weight gives steadiness, especially in breezy weather."

So we have this Lecky score card: Right: lighter-weight sextants are easier to handle; Wrong: There are women sailors, even in 1881, and some famous ones at that. Right: Heavy sextants are more stable in the wind—so long as they are sitting on the deck. Pick them up and they are without doubt more difficult to use. It is not something that must be taken on faith. A half-gallon of milk weighs 4 lbs. Just pick one up in a standing position and hold it to your nose with one hand for a few minutes watching the second hand on a clock. Then consider a 30-minute sight session, where you are holding the sextant in that way, more often than not.

Lecky's book was and still is popular because he added so much folksy dialog to his navigation text. At the end of the chapter, he advises that just like your horse, your gun, and your dog, you should never loan your sextant to anyone. He simply got a bit carried away with the sextant weight issue and forgot the science.

As a last punctuation mark to this point, one of the famous manufacturers who touted the weight virtues of its 4.6-lb brass sextants offered a rarely advertised expensive custom model made of aluminum alloy, which they claimed as the very top of the line because it was so light weight! Should we hang a piece of lead on these when taking sights in the wind? And why haven't the camera makers of the world discovered they could make more stable cameras by just increasing their weight to 4 pounds?

And in the weight department, it is the plastic sextants that win by a mile—if we can overcome their other shortcomings.

Learning sextant use

Sextant usage can be learned from a book, but if you have the opportunity, the learning might go faster with the help of an experienced navigator. You watch them; they watch you; then they check your sights just after you decide they are in alignment. In any event, sextant use is readily learned; exceptional skills and extensive training are not required. Don't worry if you have learned on land with shorelines or artificial horizons and not yet practiced at sea. Sights are often easier at sea than they are on land, even with some motion of the boat to contend with. Sextants do what they are supposed to: allow you to measure vertical angles precisely from a moving platform.

The key issue in doing practice sights is to record all measurement and environmental values. Every detail. We have found cases where the tide height was causing a discrepancy to a sight from land overlooking the water. If you keep all of your data, then you can generally figure out what went wrong if you need to. It is, after all, one of the great virtues of celestial navigation that it is so transparent. If there is an error, we can generally find it.

Preparing for sights at sea

First let us take a broad overview of the process, then come back to the crucial details.

To do sun sights, you go on deck with a sextant and your watch, along with paper and pencil to record the sights. You can do this any time the sun is up and out of the clouds, but it is best to take all sights above about 15° and below some 75° to minimize various uncertainties explained in standard texts. The sights are generally taken standing some place with good visibility and some means of support. On a sailboat, this is often on the afterdeck or amidships next to the shrouds. In rougher seas, it is best to wrap an arm around shrouds or stays during the sights—or wrap the short tether of your safety harness around the shrouds and lean back. Some system is needed to free both hands to operate the sextant while still providing support against sudden boat motion. It is difficult to imagine any reason to go forward of the mast with a sextant. If sails block your view, alter course briefly for the sight.

It would be rare to do sights sitting down. This lowers your perspective and increases chances of waves blocking your view of the true sea horizon. Also it is less stable if you are moving about. I recall once on a calm, warm, super clear night with a high moon lighting up the horizon actually doing sights sitting on the cabin top in the middle of the night, but that was one of only a couple times ever.

Before going on deck, record a log reading and corresponding watch time in a pocket size notebook you can take on deck. Also record your compass heading and knotmeter speed, or better still the COG and SOG from your GPS. This will later be used to correct the sights for boat motion during the sight session itself, which might take up to 45 minutes. Double check that no one has imminent plans to alter course significantly or to do major sail changes that might create havoc around you.

The sighting procedure begins with a check of the Index Correction (IC) by any of the methods outlined earlier, and record the results in your notebook, even if you are confirming something that has been the same forever, just write, ie IC = 1.4′ On. If anything goes wrong or is in question, it will be the first thing to suspect if you did not record something.

Sun shades

After the IC has been checked and record-ed, estimate what index shade or combination might be best to use, and rotate them to the in position. If there is bright glare on the water, add a horizon shade, but these are only used in those conditions. It is important to think of the shades as having only two locations, either all the way in, or all the way out. Each time one is changed, check that it is in the full out or full in position. Shades left partway in or out can force you to look around them in the telescope and led to false readings. This potential error is eliminated

by developing the habit of moving them full in or full out, and whenever you pick up a sextant for the first time, check that they are full out.

There is no system to the filter choice; there is also usually no logic to the layout of shades on the instrument. With 4 index shades, it could be the No.1 (count from either side) is the thinnest, then No. 3 is the next thickest, then No. 4 + No. 1 is next, and then No. 2, etc. This sequence could be anything, depending on the model. Some combinations might also lead to different colors of the sun.

If you can accept strange phraseology, the goal of shade choice is to have the sun appear as bright as possible without any impression to you of "brightness." If you put a shade combination in place and look at the sun and you have any tendency at all to consider it "bright" then try to find a combination that is just toned down from that. If on the other side, you do not see a nice sharp image of the sun, then you should go brighter. With some practice you will know what combinations work best for your sextant. On a bright clear day with a high sun, you could easily use all shades, and on some instruments maybe even want more.

The same guidelines apply to the choice of horizon shades when they are called for, which is not often, but crucial when there is glare on the water.

Taking the sight

Next face the sun and point the telescope of the sextant toward the horizon directly below the sun. Adjust the index arm of the sextant to bring the reflected view of the sun into simultaneous view with the horizon. This is done with an initial coarse movement of the arm made while squeezing the worm gear release, and then a fine adjustment with the micrometer or vernier. The final adjustment must be made when the sextant is precisely vertical, or the angle you get will be too big (Figure 2-3). With the boat heeled, rolling, and pitching, this might seem at first an impossible challenge. A simple trick, however, solves the problem.

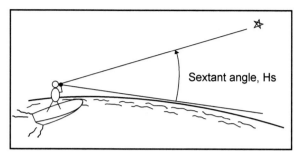

Figure 2-2 *The angle above the horizon measured by a sextant.*

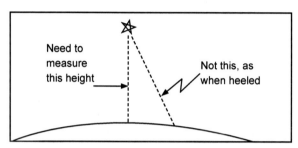

Figure 2-3 *The proper angle must be measured when the sextant is vertical. From a heeled deck or tilted sextant the angle will be too big. Rocking the sextant (Figure 2-5) is an easy way to insure this. Numerous optical gadgets have been proposed to help with this judgement, but they are not needed and just clutter up the sextant.*

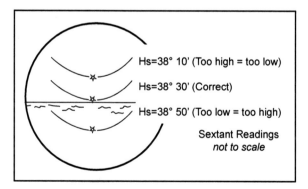

Figure 2-4 *How bodies move in the sextant telescope. You can always just turn the micrometer to learn which way the body moves, but when we are trying to control which way we turn, it can be helpful to get a feeling for this ahead of time. When the body is above the horizon, you have to increase the angle (CCW on most units) to bring it down. Hence when it is too high, it is too low—if that might help.*

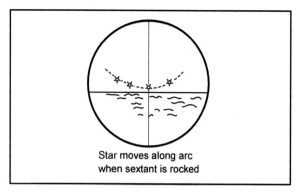

Star moves along arc
when sextant is rocked

Figure 2-5 *Rocking the sextant. This is the view from a full-horizon mirror, but we see this behavior with the sun or moon in all sextants due to reflection from the glass side, and to a lesser extent with a bright star.*

The final alignment is made while "rocking the sextant"—which means rotating it slightly to the right and then to the left (without moving the head) about an imaginary line drawn from your eye to the object as it appears on the horizon. The motion is equivalent to a gentle rolling of the sextant about its telescope axis without any yawing or pitching of the instrument as a whole. When the sextant is rocked the object viewed in the telescope will appear to swing in an arc (Figure 2-5). If the instrument begins to yaw during the roll, the object will begin to slip away from the center of the horizon glass; the job then is to adjust the heading of the sextant slightly as necessary to keep the object in view as you rock it. The sight is completed when the object just touches the horizon at the lowest point on the arc. See note in Figure 2-4 on the direction to turn.

To find the lowest arc point in an actual sight, the sextant has to be rocked only some 10° to the right and left, but a good way to learn and master the motion is to greatly exaggerate the rocking angle when practicing. This will help develop your ability to keep the object in sight during unexpected boat motions. Hold your head steady as you rock the instrument. With metal sextants, the sextant telescope rotates against your stationary cheek as you do this; with plastic instruments it is best to not have it touch your head in the process, or if so, only very lightly. If you need that contact point during the initial alignment, then remove it before checking the final reading.

Fine tune the sextant angle until you feel you have the best possible alignment of object and horizon at the lowest point of its arc and then stop further adjustments. Read your watch and record the time to the second. Don't worry about the sextant reading; it won't change. The first task is get the time recorded before you forget it. If you pause or get delayed between releasing the drum and reading the watch, estimate the few seconds it cost and adjust the time before recording it. That is, if it took you 3 seconds to read your watch (it was stuck under your cuff!) then record a time 3 seconds earlier than you read. Then read the sextant, double check the reading, and then record it along with the name of the object sighted.

Complete the round of sights, then store the sextant, and then make a final log entry into your notebook (time, course, speed). Also confirm in your notebook that the course remained constant during the sights, although you would have known of any changes during the sight session as soon as anyone, because you were watching the stars all this time.

Choice of bodies

For sun or moon sights use the bottom edge (lower limb) when available. When the lower limb is obscured by clouds use the upper limb and adjust the sextant until the top edge just skims the horizon when rocked. Sun and moon sights can be taken anytime of day they are visible and well above the horizon. Star and planet sights must be taken during twilight when both the objects and the horizon are visible. Evening star sights begin when you can first see the stars (through the sextant telescope) and they end when you can no longer discern the horizon. Morning sights begin when you can first see the horizon and they end when you can no longer see the stars. During specific periods of the year, Venus sights can be taken throughout the day.

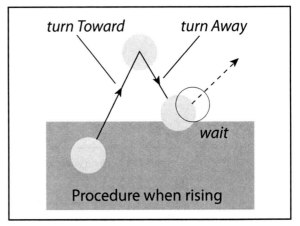

Figure 2-6 *Set and wait method when the body is rising. The last adjustment of the dial to place the body just below the horizon should be in the Away direction.*

These are fairly rare sights that require good sextant optics and very clear skies in addition to a fortuitous location of the planet.

Star or planet sights are best done by precomputing the sextant heights and bearings of the objects before the sights are taken. Then, at the twilight time used for pre-computation, set the sextant to the precomputed height and look in the precomputed direction. The object will appear near the horizon and the sight can be completed in the normal manner. Pre-computation can be carried out by standard reductions using any sight reduction tables or more readily using Pub. 249 Vol. 1 or the 2102-D Star Finder. Precomputed evening sights are easy and accurate because they can be taken early, in the brighter part of twilight while the horizon is still a sharp line. Pre-computation of morning twilight sights facilitates the actual sight taking, but is not so crucial to star ID since you have as long as you wish to study the sky while waiting for the horizon to appear. Occasionally, daytime moon sights must also be precomputed to locate a faint moon in a bright or cloudy sky.

Sight taking order

Sun and moon sights can be taken anytime they are visible. If both are visible, the order does not matter unless one is threatened to be

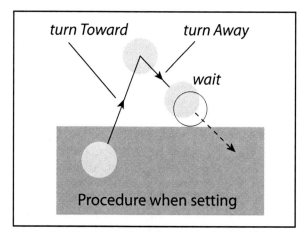

Figure 2-7 *Set and wait method when the body is setting. The last adjustment of the dial to place the body just above the horizon should be in the Away direction.*

covered by clouds, then it takes priority. Doing a sun moon fix there are advantages to alternating the sights 4 times, rather than taking 4 suns then 4 moons or vice versa. It makes it easier to figure a common time for both.

For stars, the best fix is 3 that are as near 120° apart, bright, and about the same height. Limit heights to above 15° and below 75° when possible for the best results. The low limit helps eliminate refraction uncertainties, and the upper limit rules out special corrections needed once the sights get much higher than that. Also very high sights are harder to take because it is harder to know which way to look to point at the star. Needless to say, however, you can get a fix from any stars you take, these are just the guidelines for optimizing the accuracy.

For evening sights, the logical order is take the body over the darkest part of the horizon first to extend your sight taking time, because the loss of the horizon is what stops you. Then quickly take a sight to another star so you are guaranteed of a fix. Then start alternating the sights hoping to get 3 or 4 of each body.

Inverting the sextant

When star or planet sights must be taken without pre-computation, use the special procedure of inverting the sextant. First set the scale to

0° 0', hold the sextant up-side-down in the left hand, and, while keeping the object in continuous view through the direct-view side of the glass, use the right hand to adjust the scale to bring the horizon up to the object. Once both object and horizon are in view, turn the sextant back over and complete the sight in the normal manner. This is an effective trick, and some navigators use it routinely in lieu of pre-computation, but pre-computation is a better way to choose the optimum sights and avoid redundant ones.

Set and wait method

This is the method we recommend for plastic sextant sights, primarily because it takes the least micrometer drum adjustment, so it is easier to concentrate on which way you are turning the dial on the final adjustment. It probably takes longer to do the sights this way, so it might not be so popular with metal sextant users who have established that there is little difference between the rotation direction of the drum. Nevertheless, it could improve metal sextant sights in some cases, especially in rougher seas.

The method works for any body that is rising or setting notably in your sextant view, which means it must be bearing some distance off of your meridian, or the vertical motion in your telescope might be too slow to use. If there is any doubt, just align the body with the horizon and watch to see how long it takes to notice that it is no longer in alignment. Near the equator bodies rise and set the most steeply, so this works better at lower latitudes, but it is still a good method for most sights. It would not work very well for noon sights near LAN as there is no rise or fall at that point.

For objects that are rising (i.e. bearing to the east of your meridian) get object and horizon in view, then turn the drum in the Toward direction till the object is well above the horizon, then slowly and smoothly turn the drum in the Away direction until the body is about one-eighth of a sun diameter below the horizon (some 4' or so). The goal is to get to this final waiting point by only turning in the Away direction and then stopping with no backlash on the drum.

Then do not touch the drum any longer but just wait for the sun's lower limb to rise onto the horizon as you continually rock the sextant back and forth to insure a perpendicular measurement. When the lower limb touches the horizon, note the time, and read the dial. Confirm in your notes that this was set in the Away direction.

When the body is setting, do the reverse. Turn Toward till the body is above the horizon, then carefully and slowly use the Away rotation to get the lower limb some 4' or so above the horizon and then wait for it to descend to perfect alignment. If you overshoot, just turn back Toward to get well up, then start again back down in the Away direction.

Once you have the sextant set, the rest takes only one hand, so you have the other free to hold the shrouds or whatever you are using for support. It is a comfortable, less stressful way to take a sight compared to the standard way of just turning the dials till you reach alignment. If you miss the alignment, then you have to do it again. Also, you may want to record the alignment, then watch for a few seconds to see if it is really off alignment. This way you get a rough measure of the "touch and leave" data discussed earlier. It is, however, probably best to use your first judgement of this for the sights and do not keep out-guessing yourself. If there is doubt, just rock again a few times before deciding.

Sights in rough weather

For sights in rough seas remember not to chase the object around as the boat swings around with passing seas. Once object and horizon are in view through the sextant and you have found the best direction to face the object relative to your boat (usually the direction to the object when viewed from the crests of the bigger seas of a sequence), stay oriented in that direction. As the boat rocks (yaws, rolls, and pitches) the object will go out of view, but it will return when the boat rocks back, since boat motion is typically repetitive in a seaway. Do quick, minor

adjustments while it is in view in the chosen direction, then stop when the object slips out of view but don't move, and wait for it to reappear before making further adjustments. The sights take longer—and they test your patience—but in the end they can be just as good as those taken in calmer water.

Waves will occasionally block the horizon when you are ready to make an adjustment. When this happens, you might have to skip that cycle of boat motion and wait for the next. The true horizon will appear as a smooth steady straight line, whereas intervening waves are irregular and moving. If this approach of waiting out the motion is not followed and you try to keep the object in view as the boat bounces around, false adjustments are the usual result, and the process becomes quite frustrating.

Solo vs. assisted sights

Some manuals encourage the use of an assistant for doing the sights. One person has the notebook and watch, the other drives the sextant. When the sight is in alignment, you announce "mark," and the assistant records the time. You then read the sextant and the assistant records it for you.

Seems reasonable enough, and all such manuals use the same work "mark," so it must originate in some early common reference. However, we strongly discourage this system, and recommend that you do all parts of the sight taking yourself—at least for the most part, and at least for as long as it takes to be sure you can do it all yourself.

The reasons are simple. First you may have to do it on your own one day, and this way you will be prepared. There is some choreography to the process that takes practice. Namely, where do I keep the notebook during the sights; what kind of pen works best; do I need a light to write the data, or can I use the light from the sextant; is my watch light bright enough to read at twilight; do I know which button to push to turn it on; does my cuff get in the way; how do I hold or step into the shrouds during the sights; and likely many more details. Where do I store the sextant box, once I take the sextant out of it.

Second, and equally important, if there is a mistake in the process somewhere, you do not want to consider that it was the assistant's fault. There is enough tension possible on a long ocean voyage in a small boat as it is, so there is no need to risk that. Also, what you consider clear, logical writing might not be the same as the assistant. Once a long time ago on an ocean race in need of a crucial round of sights with short time to get them, I asked for help. We did all of them and retired below only to note that they were recorded with a No.3 pencil on damp paper and were totally illegible. So if you must use an assistant, confirm readings of all the numbers and look over the writing early in the game... and then just hope they record the right time!

Use of artificial horizons

Artificial horizons simply do not work at sea. It cannot be calm enough, often enough, to even consider this a possibility. The same is true for bubble sextants. These are methods used for practice or navigation on land—the latter were developed originally for aviation. There are numerous models still available that do this job, but that is not a topic at hand.

An artificial horizon is just a reflecting surface in which you can see a reflected image of the celestial body you wish to take a sight of. You use this reflected image as the horizon in the direct view of the sextant. Then you align the reflected view from the sextant with the reflected view from the artificial horizon. You can overlap the images and do the sight reduction of all sights as if they were stars, with no dip or semidiameter corrections, or align upper limbs with lower limbs. With the latter method we must be careful with the analysis. See References for details.

An artificial horizon works quite well on land, but with certain limitations. Since the celestial body angle is doubled in the sextant, what you read on the dial as, say, 90° is actually only 45°. Thus you are limited to angles below half of your full arc range, which is typically some 60° above the horizon.

Likewise, it is difficult to do very low sights, due to the geometry of looking into the artificial horizon surface at such a low angle. Old photographs of explorers at the North Pole show them laying on the ice, as flat as they can be. It is a bit like trying to read the book titles on the bottom shelf in a bookstore when you are wearing bifocals! You can alleviate the problem by mounting your artificial horizon on a high stool, which is not a bad idea for all artificial horizon sights, but that increases the gear involved.

Davis Instruments sells a well made portable artificial horizon, modeled after early Navy versions. You can also use a plate or pan of some liquid. Mercury was the liquid of choice in the old days, but is not practical today. Water is the least effective liquid. Black motor oil works well. We have always preferred molasses—if we spill some we just lick it up.

Generally you need a high quality plate glass cover over the pan, since the *slightest* breeze will ripple the surface rendering it unusable. Molasses, on the other hand, can tolerate a very light breeze in some cases. If it sits out for a few days it gets too stiff, but a little added water and a few minutes in the microwave and you are back in business.

The guidelines to sight taking given throughout this book still apply with these sights. Please refer to the References for cautions on the altitude corrections when using upper and lower limbs and a few other nuances.

If you have water nearby, even a small lake, then chances are your practice inland will be more informative using the "dip short method" (below), rather than with an artificial horizon. But with no lakes or rivers nearby, you can definitely find out where you are with an artificial horizon. Done well, the results are as good as with a true ocean horizon. Much of the world's geography was first mapped using one.

Dip short

With access to water that presents a shoreline at least say 0.25 nmi across, then you can use that shoreline for a horizon, with only one special correction. Just take the sight in the normal way (as outlined throughout the book) and then figure as accurately as you can your height of eye (HE) above the surface.

The Dip correction to use is figured from:

$$Dip = 0.416 \times D + 0.566 \times (HE/D),$$

where HE is in feet and D is the distance from you to the shoreline directly below the body in nautical miles. The Dip correction will then be given in minutes of arc.

For example, if HE is 8.5 feet and D is 1.35 nmi, then figure the dip as: Dip = 0.416 x 1.35 + 0.566 x (8.5/1.35) = 0.562 + 3.56 = 4.1', and use this value instead of the 2.8' that you would find in the Nautical Almanac for an HE of 8.5 feet. Remember that the Dip correction is always negative, so it might be better to say, use - 4.1' instead of - 2.8'. Then do all the rest of the sight reduction in the normal way.

You do not need to worry about what direction you were looking, because that comes out of the sight reduction, but you then must go to a chart to figure D. This assumes you know where you are at the time of the sight. You can also get this from Google Earth. Refer to the References for more discussion and examples.

This can be a useful method in real navigation when you come close onto an unknown shore with no identifiable landmarks, and the only sight is the sun over the land. This calls for a measurement of your distance off an unknown landmark, which can be done by a couple methods of Part 3, or others.

Sources of accurate time

Cel nav sights require accurate time, so a first step is to be sure you know the time accurate to the second. If you do not resolve this issue right at the beginning, it will come up over and over again as a possible source of error. So nail down the time and move on.

There are numerous sources of accurate time. The easiest is www.time.gov, then go to the UTC link, and they give the time and estimated error, usually some 0.2 to 0.4 seconds. Then you might compare that time to what you get from your GPS, which should also give the right time when satellites are in view.

Probably the best is a shortwave radio tuned to WWV or WWVH (www.nist.gov, then search on wwv) for details. They give the time every minute, with a marker at the half minute and ticks on each second. The Grundig G4000A (formerly Yacht Boy 400) is a popular SW radio with sailors, on land and underway, for under $100.

In the classroom, we often fallback on a direct phone call to WWV broadcast on speaker phone so all can set their watches at once. Call

(303) 499-7111 for WWV (Colorado)

(808) 335-4363 for WWVH (Hawaii).

How to Average Celestial Sights

The beauty of celestial navigation is its transparency, meaning when we get a position fix using standard good procedures we can be completely confident that it is right, and if we make an error on the way to this fix, it is usually obvious even before we get the fix completed. With celestial navigation, we not only find our position independent of the external world, we have a way to evaluate its accuracy. This is not the case, for example, with GPS. We have to believe the GPS output based on our faith in the system, a procedure rather more appropriate to religion than to navigation. Part of the "standard good procedure" mentioned above, however, is the taking of multiple sights of each body used in the fix. If we take just one or two sights, we run the risk of starting out with less than the best possible data. These are human measurements, and we can all make an error, even in the best of conditions— an imperceptible little bump-twist of the dial, just as we release it, or some chance coincidence of the vessel's heel angle and our sextant rocking angle can lead to an imprecise sight, or just a blunder. We read the dial (of sextant or watch) as 23 and then record 32. Each of these is possible, but it is very unlikely that they would happen twice in the same series of sights.

The motivation of taking multiple sights is to average out these individual errors. Even if there were no blunders or mistakes, conventional celestial navigation is right on the edge of the ultimate capability of both man and sextant. About the best accuracy we can hope for is some ± 0.5 miles in final position, and even this level of ac-

curacy depends mostly on how we correct the process for vessel motion during the sights. And we are striving for this level of using a hand-held instrument that measures angles only to within about 0.2 miles and astronomical data that is only accurate to within about 0.1 miles. In short, to get the optimum accuracy in the final product, we must do every thing as carefully as possible.

A key question then is simply how accurate are the sights themselves? Any navigator taking multiple sights of the same body will naturally

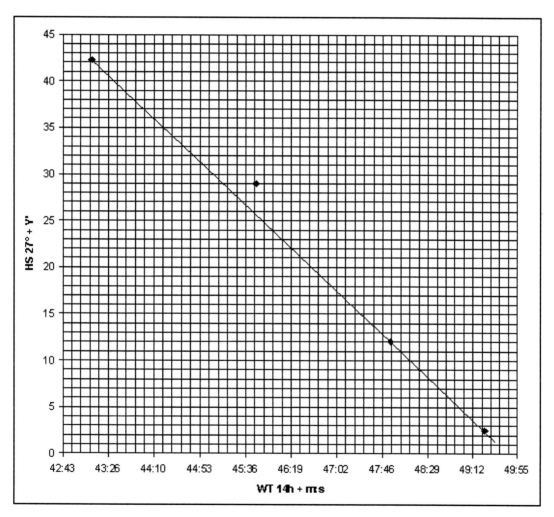

Figure 2-8 *Sextant height plotted versus time. It appears that the second sight is inconsistent with the other three.*

observe some spread in the data. The sights will not be precise, but will scatter about the proper value. The extent of the scatter is some fraction of an arc minute—maybe optimistically about ±0.2′ in ideal conditions with a good instrument in experienced hands, but more likely it will be about twice that (±0.4′) in good conditions. In poor conditions, it may be more like ±1′ or even ±2′. The question at hand here is, how do you know what that scatter is, and how do we average it out. We should note here, that even begin-

ners, after good instruction, can do a series of sights well within ±1′ in good conditions, if they take a series and average it. The use of a sextant is not a magic art, and all who care to learn can do so with only modest practice and good instruction.

The other very important point to note here is the actual extent of the scatter is not crucial to the final accuracy of the fix, assuming that it is truly random, and assuming we know how to evaluate it properly. In other words, we can get

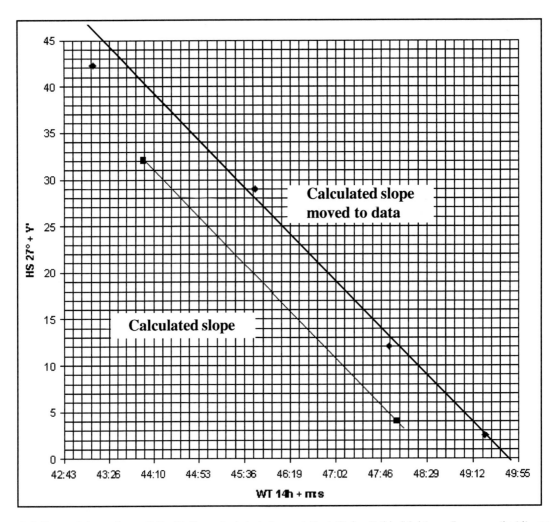

Figure 2-9 *Same data as figure 2-8 with the calculated slope plotted. Doing it this "right way" we see that it was not the second sight that was wrong, but the first one.*

just as good a fix out of sights that scatter by an arc minute or more among individual sights as we can from a set of sights that are consistent to within a few tenths of a minute of each other. And this is precisely the subject of this discussion: how to do that evaluation.

The problem is not a trivial one because the sextant height itself is changing with time, so we naturally expect each one to be different from the last one. Looking to the east, the sight angle will be getting bigger with time as the body rises, and looking west they will get smaller as the body sets. Measuring a sextant altitude for a fix is not like measuring your pulse rate, which you can just do many times in a row and then perform a simple average to get an accurate value. We must evaluate a sequence of sights and use their relative values to determine if individual ones might be in doubt. A set of sample data taken on land is shown below.

DR 47° 38′ N, 122° 20′W (Gasworks Park on Lake Union in Seattle), ZD=+8h, WE = 7s fast, HE = 7 feet. IC = 3.5′ off the scale. Sights of the sun's lower limb. Note we must use dip short for the ultimate evaluation of these sights, but that is not the issue at hand as long as the distance to the horizon does not change during the sequence.

WT	Hs
14h 43m 11s	27° 42.3′
14h 45m 46s	27° 29.0′
14h 47m 53s	27° 12.0′
14h 49m 23s	27° 02.5′

This data is plotted in Figure 2-8 to illustrate the trend.

There are two ways to average these sights for the best LOP (line of position). If you have a calculator programmed to do celestial navigation or a software product that does it on a computer, then the simplest approach is to do the sight reduction of each line from the DR position and make a list of the LOPs as follows (using HE=0):

14h 43m 11s a = 17.8′ T 221

14h 45m 46s a = 21.6′ T 221

14h 47m 53s a = 18.8′ T 222

14h 49m 23s a = 19.4′ T 222

At this point since we have removed the time dependence of the sight altitude, we can simply average the four a-values to get a = 19.4′ T 222. This would be a reasonably good way to have combined the four independent sights into one "best value." In other words, with software at hand, this is one way to "average sights." Looking at the list of LOPs and also at the plot of the Hs values, it appears that the second sight (14:45:46) is too high. It might seem reasonable to drop this one out of the list and average the rest. This would give: a = 18.7′ T 222. This is a big effect, 19.4 to 18.7 is a shift of 0.7 miles in this average LOP. We could take the attitude that our "careful" detection of one sight that was out of line has improved our accuracy by more than half a mile. In other words, computing all the a-values, noting which ones if any are well outside the other values, throwing them out and averaging the rest could be considered a second level of "sight averaging."

All of this presumes we have a calculator or software so we can sight reduce from the same assumed position a whole series of sights in a short time.

You can indeed use the same position for multiple sights with tables using Mike Peperday's *S-Tables* method, but we are not covering that here. Even if we did use tables for this analysis, it is way too long and tedious to do so for a series of sights. When we are using tables, we want to "average" the Hs values directly and then just carry out a single sight reduction on the best value sight that represents all the set.

Furthermore, we will show that the above simplified averaging of calculator solutions is not guaranteed to yield the correct result. It could well be that shifting the 19.4 to the 18.7 was a mistake. The motivation for throwing out the second sight was that it was well off the line that the other three fit onto. We assumed that nature was kind in this regard, i.e. three in a row must be right. Clearly we need some method to evaluate which sights are far enough off to be discarded, i.e. to conclude that they may be blunders or isolated errors. If a sight is say 5 miles off, it is almost certainly wrong, and if we keep it, we will be pulling the average off the proper value. So how do we proceed?

The trick is simple. We fine tune the line. In the last example, we simply took the best line that fit the most data points and drew it. It could have been any line, meaning in this case a line with any slope to it. But the trick is we know the slope. This does not have to be a free ranging option in selecting the best line. We can calculate the proper slope and then just slide that line up and down the page for the "best fit" to the data. Once we have that line in place, we have firmer ground to stand on as we pitch out some of our sights.

To calculate the slope, we do a sight reduction at some time near the beginning of the sight session to get Hc and Zn (we do not need the latter) and then do the same thing at some time near the end of the sight session. In the above example, we chose to do the computation at 14h 44m 00s to get Hc = 26° 3.3', and then again at 14h 48m 00s to get Hc = 25° 35.7'. This tells us that the sun at this time and place was setting at a rate of 63.3-35.7 = 27.6' per 4 minutes of time.

We can now draw in that line on the same plot with the data and then use parallel rules or plotter to move it up to fit the data. Just slide this line up and down to get the best fit position. There is no rotating it now for the best fit. We know that all good sights will be rising or falling at this rate. To draw the line, just choose any convenient place on the 1444 line to mark the first Hc then at 1448 mark another Hc that is 28' lower. Note that actual values of Hc used here do not matter so long as they are plotted on the right times and are 28' apart.

If we are using software, it is trivial to do these two sight reductions, it takes just a minute or two. But if we are using tables, we must do one more trick to make it work. We can't just choose two arbitrary times, since we won't be able to get a whole-degrees value of LHA for use in the tables. So we simply do it once properly from a time early in the sights or just before it (in this case 1444), and then get Hc from that, and then look up the Hc for the same declination and latitude but for an LHA which is 1° higher. This will give the Hc for 4 minutes later (1448). You can then use these two values to figure the slope. If the d-value in the sight reduction tables is the same at both LHAs, then you do not even need to figure the d-correction since that will not change the slope. Using Pub 249 for the above calculations, you get Hc at 1444 (Lat = 48° N, Dec = S 6°, LHA = 38°) = 26° 32' and at 1448 (Lat = 48° N, Dec = S 6°, LHA = 39°) = 26° 04' which gives the same 28' per 4 minutes slope that we got by computer.

Figure 2-9 shows this result applied to the sight data at hand. Note the interesting result that poor ole Sight No.2 that we were so ready to throw out was probably quite OK. The problem sight was No. 1, which looks off by more than 4' or so!

It's way too late to say "in short," but at least "in summary," this is a good trick to know about for evaluating sextant sights. It is especially valuable on those days when the electronics have failed completely and the sky has been overcast for some days and you are anxious for at least a good LOP and all you get is 3 hurried sights in broken cloud cover and choppy seas, and you have to make the best of these.

Once the data are analyzed in this manner, we then just select one sight from the good data line and sight reduce it. In this example, we could use the last sight, right on the line, or we could use sight No 2 and take 1' off the value (it was not way out of line at all!), or sight No. 3 and add 1' or use the purely fictitious sight at 47:02 with an Hs of 27° 19.0'. We did not actually measure a height at this last time, but if we had, that is most likely what we would have gotten. Any one of these sights is the proper "average" of the full set of four, *but it took the full set of four and some reasoning to pick it out.*

With some practice at this you will note that 4 sights are notably better than just 3, but you don't gain much with 5. Also, *this works best if the sights are taken promptly, or at least without long delay over the sequence.* The longer the time span of the sights, the larger the span in Hs, which makes the plot less sensitive to small differences. Spans over 20 min or so do not work well.

Also if you are moving fast and take a longer time on the sight session, then you should consider that the slope of the Hs data can be affected somewhat. To account for this calls for doing the first Hc from the DR of the first sight and the last HC from the DR of the last sight. This is easy to account for with a calculator solution, but more work with tables. It is usually not a factor for a routine set of sunlines at typical yacht speeds, in which case you can do the 4 sights in 5 or 6 minutes.

Celestial Sights with Plastic Sextants

This short section is a central point of the book, in that it summarizes those steps required to get the most accuracy and dependability from plastic sextants. The steps are here; the details are spread throughout the book. Needless to say, for any sextant, you will always get the best results if you choose the optimum sights and sight times. This means choosing star planet triads carefully and doing solar running fixes centered on LAN when possible.

Step 1

Measure the IC values as explained earlier. Use both the Toward and Away methods till you appreciate the differences, then concentrate on doing all IC measurements and sights in the Away direction—or more specifically, to cover all models, in the direction of increasing sextant angle.

The sextant should be in thermal equilibrium with the ambient temperature to the best you can achieve. More to the point, avoid sudden changes in temperature just before sight taking. If you have a long set of sights to take, consider having a shaded place for the sextant during breaks.

Step 2

Use the "Set and Wait" procedure for taking the sights themselves whenever possible.

Step 3

Do at least 4 or 5 sights of each body using the Away direction. As noted earlier, 4 is very much better than 3. In normal conditions, the sights take just a few minutes each, so this is not a burden.

Step 4

Analyze your data using the Fit Slope Method covered earlier to choose the best sight of the lot for your fix. There is no need to sight reduce all of them if you are doing it by hand, just the best fit or a representative one. The slope analysis will essentially pile all the statistics of the set into that one sight.

Remember, too, that when you compute the Hc values for the theoretical slope of the line over the time range of your sights that you must use the proper DR position for each computation if they are different. When moving at any significant speed, this means updating the DR used at each computation. Sailing south at 8 kts, for example, any two sights of the same body taken more or less to the south that are 30 minutes apart in time would be some 4' different in sextant height. We must account for this in the slope analysis.

Summary and sight reduction notes

As a broad generalization, using these procedures one should be able to routinely obtain accuracies of some 5 or 6 miles with a tested plastic sextant. Maybe better in some cases (we have many examples), maybe a bit worse in others (we also have examples). Naturally, one needs to follow the good procedures outlined above to obtain good fixes.

Another step in the direction of more accurate results is to use a calculator or software program for the analysis, as opposed to doing it all by hand. You can certainly do it all by hand, and just as accurate in the end if you are very careful, but it will take much longer. In any program worth its salt, every fix is a running fix, which corrects each sight for the course and speed. You can do more sights this way, and the results for individual sight reductions will be more accurate than say Pub 249 would be.

The main improvement by calculator solution is you can reduce the sights from your best DR position and not have to use an assumed position. This makes all of the lines on the chart much shorter and alleviates some of the unavoidable approximations that go into the all paper and plotting solution. The higher the sights, the more important this is. Please refer to a cel nav text for the details. Generally these are all small effects (computer vs. tables), but when you want to do the very best, we have to optimize everything. We could easily give up ±0.5' or more in unfavorable cases.

In any event, if your fix position comes out more than 50 nmi off of your DR position, then you are best to call that fix your new DR and do the sight reduction once again. This is even true with some calculators that (mathematically) intersect two LOPs for a fix instead of the more correct way of intersecting two COPs. These details are beyond this book.

If you are using a program or calculator with an internal nautical almanac, then it is also crucial to check that its almanac is correct. Use the data from the USNO Astronomical Applications website for the standard if you do not have a printed government almanac.

This level of plastic-sextant accuracy is to be compared with that obtainable routinely from metal sextants—also requiring good procedures and analysis—of some 1 or 2 miles depending on conditions. The big difference is you can push the metal sextant accuracy to ±0.5 nmi with care and good skill, but we would have to consider getting some ±2 nmi from a plastic sextant as the top of the line in skill and procedures.

Specific sights are presented next as background to these conclusions. The results are not optimized. They could have been improved by following the instruction presented here, but these data remain valuable as documented measurements done without optimizing the procedures. Though we have taught various forms of these methods for years, the actual formulation of the ideas as presented in this book now were developed during these sights and subsequent analysis. The work was originally motivated in large part by our early 90's correspondence with Cruising World Magazine—a motivation which they further kindled by their thoughtful response to our comments and concerns. Hopefully the article they published and the response they generated from it motivated more navigators to get involved with celestial navigation. It is an enjoyable and rewarding pastime.

The recent publication of Bruce Stark's work on lunar distance (covered later) has also generated a resurgent interest in celestial navigation. For those who want to do the very best they can with sextants, metal or plastic, lunar distance is the way to do it. You can practice from a chair in your backyard, and when you master lunars your routine cel nav will be on par with the very best.

Plastic Vs. Metal Sextant Results

In the Appendix there is a detailed description of a series of sights with plastic and metal sextants. These details are crucial to understanding the factors that contribute to final results. All the data are there, so they can be reanalyzed as desired. The notes illustrate several points mentioned throughout the book.

We did sun and moon sights underway and on land using metal and plastic sextants. The results are summarized in the table here. Each of the average intercepts listed in the table of averages below represent 4 or more sights. The sun-moon sights were used for running fixes. No special analysis (such as slope fitting) was applied. The averages include all sights taken. All can be improved with more careful analysis.

The intercepts (a-values) were computed taking into account the course and speed of the vessel when underway. The Assumed Positions used were our best estimate of the true positions at the time of each sight, based on DR between a recorded GPS position before and after each sight session. In that sense, the intercepts are a measure of the accuracy of the sights. In a couple cases, running fixes were calculated.

The sights were taken in what must be considered random micrometer drum directions, because at the time we did not appreciate the superiority of the Away (CCW) direction for improved accuracy—we did not cut open the Davis sextant till the preparation of this book. We were well aware that CW and CCW gave big plastic sextant differences in IC and this was measured and noted, but we effectively averaged these to use in the analysis. Thus these data represent a good measure of what might be called doing plastic sextant sights in the common manner. We obviously had not read the Davis manual carefully, either, as it specifically states you should use the Away (increasing angle) direction. The IC data presented, however, does support the result that the Away direction is superior.

Set	Summary of Averages*	
1.	Metal underway moon	0.9' T ± 1.7
1a.	Metal underway sun	0.1' A ± 1.3
4.	Metal underway sun	1.6' T ± 0.4
6.	Metal on land sun	0.5' A ± 0.6
2.	Mark 15 underway sun	6.7' A ± 1.4
2a.	Mark 15 underway moon	4.3' A ± 1.4
5.	Mark 15 underway sun	5.1' A ± 1.0
3.	Mark 3 underway moon	8.4' T ± 2.5
3a.	Mark 3 underway sun	5.8' T ± 2.5
7.	Mark 15 on land sun	4.0' A ± 2.3
8.	Mark 3 on land sun	1.6' T ± 1.6

See Appendix for details. Each set has multiple sights, with all IC measurements included.

The sights are from July, 2000 during the Victoria, BC to Maui, HI yacht race. Sights were all taken by the author under spinnaker in trade wind conditions, surfing in 8 to 10 foot seas with speeds varying from 7 to 14 kts and headings varying some ±20° or so—not ideal conditions for celestial sights, but still doable, which is one of the points we wanted to make with these data. The sun was bright and very hot, which was a factor underway and it was even very much hotter during the sights on land that followed.

We had to assume that the "true positions" were uncertain by as much as ±0.5 mi or so, but very likely not any more than that. You will see in the details that the intercept labels for the metal sextant were randomly A and T (unfortunately a different meaning of these terms), which implies no systematic error, but we did see definite systematic errors in some plastic IC sights.

Hopefully the data help make our point about plastic sextant sights. It took a lot of time to document what we and many others knew is true without these examples. There are also numerous accounts elsewhere, both documented and anecdotal, that support the conclusion that a properly used plastic sextant can get consistent fixes within 5 or 6 miles by averaging multiple sights, even if each of the sights themselves may be off by this amount or even more—and even in the burning sun for the period of the sight session. Our recent work with plastic sextant lunars and solar IC method using Baader filters, encourages us to propose that with care you might do even notably better than that. Though not documented here, the limits of practical metal sextant fixes at sea remains about ±0.5 nmi (done with best procedures and properly analyzed), with routine good results being closer to ±1 or 2 nmi, depending on conditions and time spent on analysis.

Lunar Distance

Routine celestial navigation relies upon accurate time (Universal Time) to find the longitude of a position (latitude does not require time). Advanced celestial navigators, however, can find longitude without knowing the time using the technique of lunar distance, or "lunars" for short. In this technique, the sextant is used to measure the angular distance between the moon and another celestial body along its path, as shown in Figure 2-10. Since this distance slowly changes as the moon moves eastward though the zodiac constellations, it can be used to find the time of day that is needed to complete the longitude determination, as illustrated in Figure 2-11. Lunar skills have long been considered the hallmark of the very best celestial navigators.

There are several reasons this valuable technique has not been part of routine celestial navigation for over a hundred years. First and foremost, it is not needed, so long as the navigator has accurate time, which is readily at hand these days in routine conditions. We have accurate time from every GPS satellite, and there are numerous radio broadcasts of GMT, now called Universal Time (UT). But it is not unheard of, nor unimaginable to lose track of the time, or even the day. And prudent good seamanship means considering things beyond normal conditions.

Nevertheless, the main reason most navigators do not do lunars is they have accurate time and do not need to—that is, if we rule out the even bigger reason, namely, most navigators do not know the technique exists. It was not covered in any books they used.

Navigators who are aware of lunars and would like to learn them have had other challenges. First, the special diagonal sextant sights are more difficult than normal cel nav sights, which are always measured straight up from the horizon, and the results must be more accurate. This requires learning to use the sextant to its very limits, which is usually implied to be metal

alone. But this challenge is part of the reward. The practical limit to metal sextant accuracy is about ±0.1' of arc. Without much practice or good instruction, navigators might average some 3 or 4 times that limit, or even a bit worse. To be successful with lunars, however, you must practice until you can approach the instrument limit routinely, even using the sextant in the awkward diagonal manner. Higher-powered monocular telescopes help with this. Precomputing the lunar distance ahead of time is also helpful.

We can, however, do lunars with plastic sextants, but this takes even more care, and average results are not as good as with metal sextants. Put another way, it would make you an even better navigator if you could do them with plastic sextants, and in any event it is a way to see how the whole process works without the investment in a metal sextant. Our goal here is to outline a few points that will help with this endeavour.

The other issue that has limited the number of practicing "lunarians" has been the challenge of analyzing the lunar distance to get longitude once it has been measured accurately. The government tables that used to do this went out of print in the early 1900s and it is essentially impossible to use old ones for modern sights. There are computer programs and Internet sites that have computed the solutions for many years, but reliance on a computer or an Internet service for a back up procedure is completely incongruous. Thus there has not been a logical role for lunars outside of academic and historic study beyond a select group of sextant experts who use it to maintain their prowess. That is, until now.

The solution is a recently republished book called the *Stark Tables for Clearing the Lunar Distances*. It has been well received by experts in this field and promises to rekindle interest in this venerable technique. Earlier editions of the book were difficult to locate, but now it is readily available from any book store.

Doing all the paperwork by hand, filling out custom forms, you can go from a measured lunar distance to the correct time and your longi-

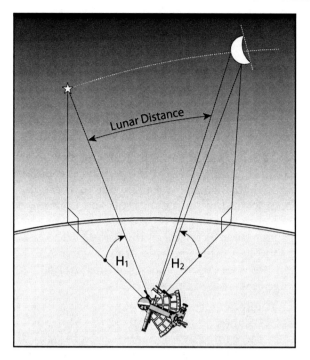

Figure 2-10. *"Lunar distance" is the angle between the edge of the moon and another celestial body along the Zodiac. The sextant can reach out to about 120°, though sights half this range or less are easier to do. The angular heights of the bodies perpendicular to the horizon (H1 and H2) are used in the analysis, but these values can be computed if an almanac is available.*

tude in about 15 minutes, without even needing a calculator.

You can measure the lunar distance any time of night that is convenient, since you do not need to see the horizon. The altitudes of the bodies above the horizon (which cannot be seen in the middle of the night) are needed in the process, but they can be computed from tables to sufficient accuracy from a DR position. Likewise, the sun and moon are frequently in good view for the sights throughout the day.

The time or longitude accuracy achievable by lunar distance depends on the quality of the sights and the choice of bodies. *The Stark Tables* explain how to choose the best companion body. You want one in line with the motion of the moon, so the change in lunar distance with time is the greatest. The sun is good just about any time it is in view with the moon and within reach of the sextant. At night you want bodies (star or planet) perpendicular to a line drawn across the horns of the moon. It can be on either side. *The Stark Tables* include a way to evaluate the quality of your choice in this regard, and they also provide detailed instructions on taking the sights.

You can't expect to get lunar longitudes as precise as you can with accurate time, but they will be quite serviceable. A 1 arc minute sextant

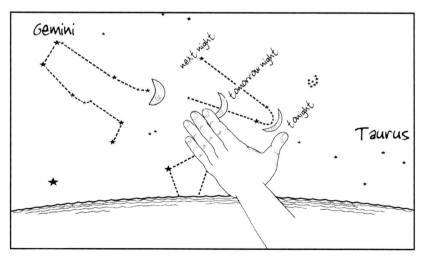

Figure 2-11. *The moon circles the earth (360°) in about 30 days, so viewed at the same time each night, the moon moves eastward through the stars at a rate of about 12°/day. The moon's path is through the stars of the Zodiac. Drawing from* Emergency Navigation *by David Burch.*

error (1.0′) in the distance measurement will cause about a 2 minute error in the time when using the best companion bodies. If you can achieve 0.5′ accuracy, you improve to 1 minute error in time, which corresponds to a 15′ error in longitude. This in turn corresponds to about 15 nmi in the Tropics or about 10 nmi at the latitude of Seattle. Navigators skilled in this method can generally get down to averaging closer to 30 seconds error in time.

If you surf around the web looking into the topic online, you will find far more discussion of the details and complexities of the process than you will find discussion of its practical use today. And sure enough, there are many nuances to the process. These details, however, are all accounted for in *The Stark Tables*, so they can be treated as we do so many other navigation tables. Just use them for their practical value without worrying about the rigors of their physical and mathematical foundations. In the end the test is very simple. You stand at a known place with a watch set to some unknown error, and see if you can find out where you are. If it works for you there, it will work for you at sea. It is one of the most rewarding navigation exercises you can do.

With *The Stark Tables* in your nav station, you no longer have to fear losing power to your electronic navigation aids, nor are you dependent on accurate time from any official broadcast. It is a small investment in time and energy that greatly expands your skills and preparation for the unexpected. Indeed, if you cared to print out even a relatively modest set of pre-computed lunar distances, you could sail worldwide for 20 years without any contact with or requirements from civilization. The lunar altitudes would have to be measured in this scheme because Long Term Almanacs do not cover the moon or planets.

For practice doing lunars and for precomputed lunar distances, see Frank Reed's excellent lunar web site listed in the References. He provides a way to get an instant solution to the lunar distance as well as a way to confirm that you have used the Stark Tables correctly.

Example 1

July 6, 2010, location 47° 40.5′N, 122° 23.9′W. Watch Error = 3s fast. ZD = +7, Davis Mark 15 (20+ years old). Before the sights, the IC and side error were set to zero as best as possible using overlapping moons. Then we get the error analysis from computed lunar distances using IC = 5.0′ Off.

The IC was measured applying the "solar method" to the daylight moon with the sextant rotated to measure the diameter of the moon from lower limb to upper limb and then upper to lower, 3 times. (We had not developed the Baader solar filters yet at this time.) The spread in the few measurements done is large (±3.2′) but the error in the final value must not be that large at all, based on our results.

The difference between sum of On and sum of Off divided by number of sights (6) is the IC, then the sum of the On sum and Off sum divided by 2 times number of sights (12) is equal to the SD of the moon. The result is IC = 5.0 Off and the measured SD is 14.7. The actual value at the time was 15.3′ so this reflects the errors in the methods. With these sights, the sun was too bright to use for IC, and attempts at horizon IC did not yield consistent results. If we had had a Baader filter at the time, we would have almost certainly got better data on the IC.

The average result is relatively good, showing that one can use a plastic sextant for this type of measurement with care. All the sights including the IC were done rotating the micrometer drum in a counterclockwise direction, which I thought of as the Away direction. If any time it seemed that this was an over-adjustment, I would back off and come back to it again in that direction. There is no proof here that this made a difference, but that is how it was done.

Example 2

The lunar distance to Venus was measured at about 10 pm local time, July 15, 2010 from a location of approximately 47° 40.5′N, 122° 24.5′W. Watch Error = 0. ZD = +7, to make the

A. Mark 15 IC measurement for Lunar Example 1		
#	On	Off
1	27.0	60 - 28.0 = 32.0
2	25.0	60 - 27.4 = 32.6
3	21.0	60 - 21.5 = 38.5
	sum = 73.0	sum = 103.1
	+103.1	-73.0
	= 176.1	= 30.1
	176.1 / 12 = 14.7	30.1 / 6 = 5.0 off
	Moon SD = 15.3	

B. Mark 15 IC measurement for Lunar Example 1			
#	On	Off	IC	SD
1	27.0	32.0	2.5 Off	14.8
2	25.0	32.6	3.8 Off	14.4
3	21.0	38.5	8.8 Off	14.9
		AVG =	5.0 Off	14.7

Early writing on this technique suggest adding all On and all Off data and then figuring the averages to get the IC as in Table A. But since we can use the measured value of the SD as a check on each set, it seems best to take advantage of that, and consider discarding ones that do not look good and have a bad SD, as in Table B. In this Example 1, however, we learn nothing from this distinction. In the Example 2, however we do, and we get improved results.

The results in Table C are computed lunar distances.

C. Lunars with a Mark 15, Example 1				
#	Watch Time	Lunar Distance	LD error	Lon error	Time error
1	13h 25m 16s	64° 17.2'	-0.5'	14' E	056s Slow
2	13h 26m 38s	64° 18.4'	+1.3'	40' W	160s Fast
3	13h 28m 03s	64° 15.6'	-0.8'	25' E	100s Slow
4	13h 29m 49s	64° 14.4'	-1.2'	37' E	148s Slow
5	13h 32m 08s	64° 14.2'	-0.4'	12' E	048s Slow
	AVG =		-0.3'	10' E	040s Slow

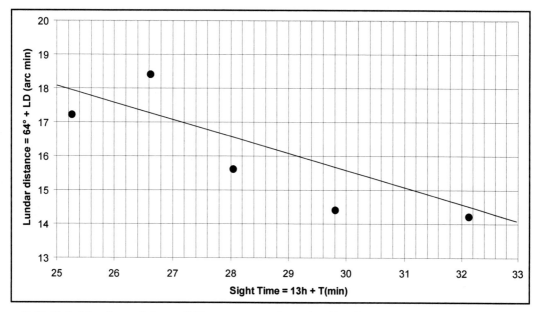

Figure 2-12 *Plot of five lunar distance (LD) measurements made with a Mark 15 plastic sextant. The solid line is the correct slope of the LD, which we can compute for any case. The plot implies that the second sight is not consistent with the others, which is borne out by the analysis.*

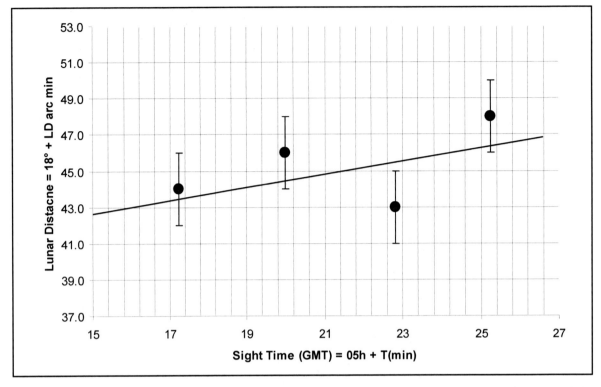

Figure 2-13 *Four lunar distance (LD) measurements made with a Mark 3 plastic sextant, modified to use a Mark 15 telescope. The solid line is the true theoretical slope of the computed LD. The plot implies the third sight is not consistent with the others, which is borne out by the analysis.*

IC measurement for Lunar Example 2		
#	On	Off
1	25	60 - 18 = 42
2	24	60 - 20 = 40
3	20	60 - 18 = 42
	IC	Moon SD
1	8.5 off	16.8
2	8.0 off	16.0
3	11.0 off	15.5
Avg	8.3 off	16.4

Lunars with a Mark 3, Example 2					
#	Watch Time	Lunar Distance	LD error	Lon error	Time error
1	05h 17m 15s	18° 44'	-0.1'	3' E	012s Slow
2	05h 19m 59s	18° 46'	+0.5'	16' W	064s Fast
3	05h 22m 49s	18° 43'	-3.9'	116' E	464s Slow
4	05h 25m 14s	18° 48'	-0.1'	2' E	008s Slow
	AVG =		+0.1'	4' W	015s Fast

UT of sights at about 05z on the 16th. The sextant was a Davis Mark 3, modified to use a Mark 15 scope as shown in Figure 2-14. The IC and side error were set to zero as best as possible using overlapping moons. Then we get the error analysis by comparing with the computed lunar distances using IC = 8.3' Off.

IC was measured using upper and lower limb of the moon at the end of the sight session, which was near vertical at sight time. The data are shown below. We could look up the SD of the moon and it was 16.3', so the obvious set of data in error was not counted in the average. The difference between sum of On and sum of Off divided by 2 is the IC, then the sum of the On sum and Off sum divided by 4 is equal to the SD of the moon. The result is IC = 8.3' Off not counting the last measurement which is inconsistent with the first two. Note that the 6 IC measurements took longer than the 4 lunar distance sights.

The average result is very good. Even the individual results are very good ruling out the one

sight that was definitely off by inspection alone. We will need to do more sights with this rig to learn how much luck was involved with these measurements. They were taken from a comfortable seated position, and not hurried, but still considering how difficult it is to read the vernier these are exceptional results.

Please refer to Part 1 on the care that must be exercised in using and reading the Mark 3. A light with magnifying glass and patience is called for.

The main point to be made here is that these sights are indeed feasible with plastic sextants. The exercise prepares you for an emergency loss of GMT and it also provides an engaging look into the way cel nav was done in the past. The book *Stark Tables for Clearing the Lunar Distance* is a way to solve for GMT and longitude without relying on computers or web sites. It is a wonderful resource.

Several other examples and testimonials are in the Appendix for both altitude measurements and lunars. Figure 2-15 shows how lunar distances change with time.

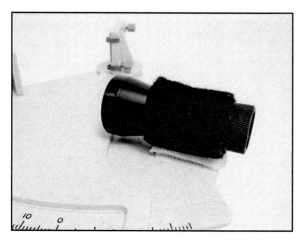

Figure 2-14 *A Davis Mark 3 sextant with a telescope from a Davis Mark 15. The scopes sell for $20 from Davis Instruments as a replacement part. The sighting tube on the Mark 3 was cut off and then the arc filed to flat. Then two layers of adhesive Velcro were applied to the arc to mount the scope. Two were needed to raise the clearance for the index arm to pass under it. Adhesive Velcro wrapped on the scope provides the connection. Be sure the Velcro does not interfere with the focusing.*

This arrangement has worked very well for celestial altitudes and lunars. Occasionally horizontal sextant sights for piloting work best without a scope, in which cases a sighting tube can be rigged with Velcro to easily replace the telescope as needed.

Computed Lunar Distances, July 16, 2010										
UTC	0:00	1:00	2:00	3:00	4:00	5:00	6:00	7:00	8:00	9:00
Sun	58° 03.8'	58° 37.6'	59° 11.5'	59° 45.3'	60° 19.1'	60° 52.8'	61° 26.6'	62° 00.3'	62° 34.0'	63° 07.6'
change	33.8'		33.8'		33.7'		33.7'		33.6'	
Venus	16° 19.7'	16° 51.2'	17° 22.9'	17° 54.6'	18° 26.4'	18° 58.2'	19° 30.1'	20° 02.0'	20° 34.0'	21° 06.0'
change	31.5		31.7'		31.8'		31.9'		32.0'	

Figure 2-15. *Computed lunar distances shows what we are up against in these measurements. The change value is how much the distance changes per hour, which is about 0.5'/min, and these are good conditions. Choose the wrong body and it is worse. Computed from Frank Reed's Lunar web site.*

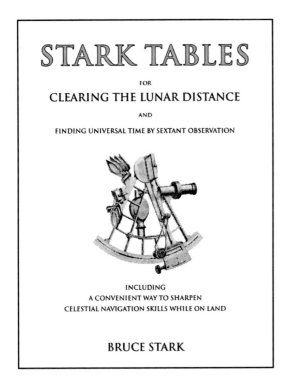

Figure 2-16. *For those who wish to pursue lunar distance, this excellent book provides a lunar solution that does not rely on a computer or calculator. It offers a one book backup solution to the loss of GMT and all electronics underway. It is an innovative solution praised by modern experts as both practical and an insight into how navigation proceeded in the early days of navigation.*

Sextant Piloting

Role in Modern Navigation

Although sextants were originally invented for lunar distance, they quickly became the instrument of choice for all celestial sights. It also became clear very early on that they were the navigator's best tool for piloting. Within the first few years of sextant use in the mid 1700s, there were articles in the Philosophical Transactions in London stressing that it was still not being used enough for piloting:

> "There is no instrument so well adapted to many kinds of piloting, either for exactness or convenience... but also with a much greater degree of precision, than can be hoped for by any other means, as it is the only instrument in use, in which neither the exactness of the observations, nor the ease with which they may be taken are sensibly affected by the motion of the vessel; and hence a single observer in a boat, may easy determine the situation of any place he pleases, to twenty or thirty feet upon every three or four miles."

This evaluation remains as true today as it did in 1765 when it was written. The GPS we all depend upon is a two-edged sword. When it is working, it is a blessing that immensely enhances our navigation, not just in position fixing, but in the more important role of telling us what direction we are going and how fast we are

doing it. When it is not working, we are left to our own wits and wisdom to find our way. And if the convenience of the GPS had led us to slack off on this learning, we can get into trouble in a hurry.

And now we learn that the GPS may not be so bulletproof as we might hope. Recent examples of the loss of one of just two WAAS satellites and studies showing the general vulnerability of GPS to jamming and solar flares may be warning signs we should heed. Also the fact that so many nations are now building or renovating competing GPS systems must be a flag that someone feels there is need for back up or alternatives.

Looking ahead, there is every reason to believe that basic navigation skills, such as precision sextant piloting, will indeed have a place in our lives once again. To march foreword ignoring this is not prudent.

Another reason sextant piloting comes back to mind these days is the awareness that you do not need an expensive metal sextant to do it. You can do it all and with amazing precision with a Davis Mark 3 plastic sextant that is actually quite durable in this application. The current list price is $59, but they often appear in sailor's swap meets, or on sale, for less.

Needless to say, you can do it with a high-quality metal sextant, and whenever the angles are very small they are better done that way, but the bulk of the methods work fine with a simple plastic sextant, and some of the workhorse techniques are actually easier with a Mark 3 than with a full-sized metal sextant—mainly because the metal sextants are all much heavier.

Sextant piloting means finding out where you are from angles you measure with a sextant. Unlike sextant use in celestial navigation, we are now using all terrestrial targets and we must have a chart showing these targets for most applications.

There are two categories: vertical angles and horizontal angles. In both categories, you find a circle of position (COP) from the sextant sight, rather than a line of position (LOP) that you would find from a compass bearing or natural range. The intersection of two COPs or one COP and one LOP gives a position fix.

Vertical Angles

Your distance from a landmark (the radius of a COP) can be determined from vertical sextant angles three ways. If the landmark is shown on a chart, then you can use the result for chart navigation. If not, you are just finding your distance to it, wherever it is. For all vertical-angle methods you need to know your height of eye above the water (HE) at the location where you take the sight.

The earliest records of navigators using vertical angles dates from the very beginnings of navigation in the 1400s, when navigators started recording landmark elevations to be used for this propose in journals that evolved into what we now call Coast Pilots. Angles were then measured with a quadrant or some form of a kamal. The peak of writing about these techniques came in the mid to late 1800's, then we read gradually less and less till modern times when these methods are rarely mentioned at all in textbooks.

Method 1 (close)

Measure the vertical angle between the top of an object whose height you know and the waterline at the object. Then with this measured angle

(α) and the known height of the object (H) you can figure your distance to the object (D) from a set of tables or by direct computation. The table needed is Bowditch Table 16, which is available online as a pdf, along with a numerical calculator for the distance. See www.starpath.com/navpubs for a free download of both. The calculator solutions are the most convenient. The equations are presented in the Appendix. The Bowditch online version has a section that explains the mathematics of all its tables.

This is the most basic of the methods. We can use it to find distance to a peak, or distance to a vessel whose mast height we know. This is for closer targets whose waterlines are in sight, below the visible horizon line. You can get a good estimate of the distance to the visible horizon line in nautical miles from the square root of HE in feet. If your eye is 9 feet above the water, then the horizon cuts off your view at about 3.0 nmi. So if your answer turns out to be more than 3 miles (meaning you are not seeing the true base of the object because it is cut off by the curvature of the earth), then you need to use the analysis of Method 2. Same measurement data, just different analysis. The methods are illustrated in Figure 3-1.

In Method 1, we assume that HE is very small compared to both D and H, and thus it does not enter into the distance-off analysis; it is just used to gauge the valid range we can work within. The resulting distance we compute is then the distance to the peak itself, not to the waterline we actually used, which will be closer to us. When you draw a COP from the measurement, it should be centered at the peak of the target.

Whenever Method 1 is valid, you can use an approximate solution for quick estimates. Use

$$D = H/100/\alpha.$$

D is in nmi, H in feet, and α in decimal degrees. When α is less than about 15° and HE is much less than H, then your distance to an object in nmi is just the height of the object in hundreds of feet divided by the angle in degrees.

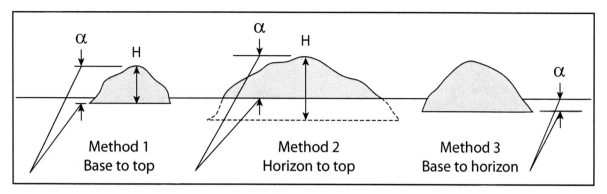

Figure 3-1. *In these sketches, α marks the angular height that is measured with a sextant and H is the charted elevation of the object. As an example for Method 1, H = 480 ft, α = 5.5°, HE = 9 ft, then the Bowditch calculator for Table 16 gives D = 0.82 nmi. The quick approximation gives 4.8/5.5 = 0.87 nmi. If H=900 ft and α = 1.2° with HE = 9 ft, we would get an approximate answer of 9/1.2 = 7.5 nmi, which is well beyond our horizon estimated at square-root (9) = 3 nmi, which implies we need to use Bowditch Table 15 calculator (Method 2) to get D = 6.7 nmi. If we can see an islet or vessel, waterline notably below the horizon, we can figure the distance to it from the angular width of that gap using Method 3. For example, α = 0° 40' and HE = 9 ft, then from Bowditch Table 17 calculator we learn the object is D = 241 yards away. To avoid interpolation, the calculators are better than the printed tables (www.starpath.com/navpubs). They will run in a smart phone. Equations needed to program your own are given in links provided in the Appendix.*

The Appendix shows how this approximation follows from the correct solution.

And you can go on—use another approximation that 1 cm spans 1° at arm's length (which we call 57 cm), and then you can measure the angles with a small ruler for quick estimates of distance off of known objects, as shown in Figure 3-2.

Without a ruler, we can use finger widths, which span about 1.5° each. These makeshift applications and how to "calibrate" your fingers are discussed in the book *Emergency Navigation*. For example, from where you are standing, measure the height of a window across the street in finger widths, then use a sextant to measure it exactly so you can determine how wide your finger is. Then after a few cross checks, you are walking around with a sextant in (on) your hand at all times!

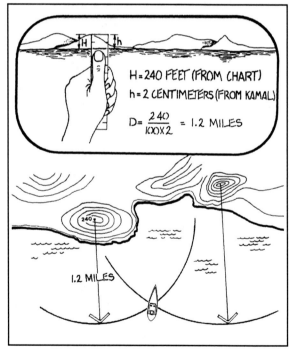

Figure 3-2. *Using a ruler as a makeshift sextant to measure the angular height of a hill. This is a modern version of ancient Arabic Kamal, used to navigate the East Coast of Africa following the monsoon winds up and down the coast. Illustration from the book* Fundamentals of Kayak Navigation. *Top of the ruler is aligned with top of the object, and top of the thumb marks the shoreline below it. See also* Emergency Navigation.

Method 2 (far)

When the base of the object is below your horizon, use Table 15 or its corresponding calculator. For target bases just over the horizon, this gives much the same answer as Method 1, but for the extreme cases when we just see the tip of a mountain on the horizon (α being a very small angle), it is crucial to use Method 2 and be sure the sextant's Index Correction (IC) and your HE are accurate. This can be a valuable observation at the first sight of land after an ocean passage. It will be the first time you know if your GPS was right!

For practice before heading off to sea, use any distant hill seen over a lake or bay shoreline. As long as the shoreline is farther off (in nmi) than the square root of your eye height (in ft) it is being cut off by the curvature of the earth. If you do not have topo maps or charts that identify the peaks, try Google Earth, which can be quite remarkable for this.

This example is pushing the method to its limits. The horizon was not good and the peaks on the horizon took some work to identify. More typical applications on a voyage are easier. The HE in these sights was 21 ft. The peak is Mt Constance at 7735 ft, located 29.7 nmi away. A metal sextant measurement ($\alpha = 2° 17.2'$) told us we were 29.2 nmi off, which is quite good in that our horizon was not super sharp.

With our Mark 3 that has a Mark 15 telescope, we got 2° 6' with a solar IC of 10' Off, to yield $\alpha = 2°16'$, which gives 29.2 nmi off. The plastic sextant will clearly do the job for Method 2 measurements. (For angles much below 1°, however, a metal sextant would yield more dependable results.)

Both sights were averages of 4 sights, but none varied much from the average. The plastic IC solar measurement, however, took much longer than the actual peak height measurement.

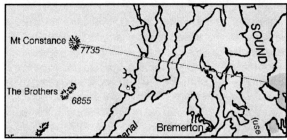

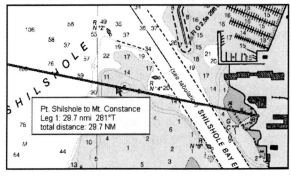

Figure 3-3. *Top. View across Puget Sound to the Olympic mountains from an eye height of 21 ft. Tallest peak in view here is Mt Constance, which is also shown on chart 18007. The location of the sight taking is shown below on Chart 18447. The echart distance was measured using Memory-Map Navigator and free echarts from NOAA.*

Figure 3-4 shows a landfall or departure view taken from old Sailing Directions—sadly these types of pictures are not included in the new US editions, but remain in the British Admiralty versions. These would be the views at the times you might use the vertical sextant angle to establish your distance off. If it does not agree with your GPS, you may have discovered a new land!

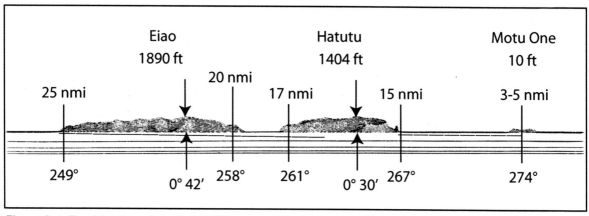

Eiao
1890 ft

Hatutu
1404 ft

Motu One
10 ft

25 nmi   20 nmi   17 nmi   15 nmi   3-5 nmi

249°   0° 42'   258°   261°   0° 30'   267°   274°

Figure 3-4. *Two islands and atoll in the NW group of the Marquesas. The sketch is from a 1990s* Sailing Directions, Pub 206, *described as 16 nmi off, looking "toward 264T," but we do not know for certain what target was at that bearing. They had to be fairly close to Motu One to see it at all.*

We added the annotations (all approximate) and looked up the elevations. We assume the height of eye is 15 ft, based on chart standards listed in the publication, which was used in computing the estimated vertical sextant angles shown. From this distance off, only about 100 ft of the Hatutu elevation was below the horizon. The banks of both islands are very steep. With a real bearing measurement and a sextant height, we could get a precise fix from this view of the horizon. All values here are estimated.

Jack London taking a sextant sight from the Cruise of the Snark. *On June 6, 1908 they departed Suva in Fiji bound for Port Resolution, due west, on Tanna Island, Vanuatu. He needed to clear the isolated 2000-ft flat-topped volcanic island of Futuna, 42 nmi east of Tanna, which he did do remarkably as planned, but with much anxiety in light of the struggles he had teaching himself celestial navigation underway. He had just a day earlier learned how to figure his longitude. The books he used were* Bowditch *and* Lecky, *the latter of which taught him what we call here Method 2. He used it to find he was 9.3 nmi off*

as he passed. Assuming an eye height of about 9 feet, his corrected sextant angle must have been about 1° 57'. Those interested in learning more of celestial navigation will enjoy the book, and be grateful that we have much easier ways to do it and to teach it today.

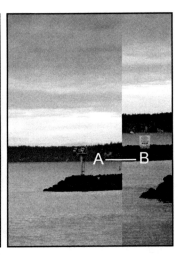

Figure 3-5. *Using Method 3 to find distance to the breakwater. The HE was 21 ft, the angle α can be measured two ways, either A to B, where we consider the breakwater (B) the horizon and bring the distant shoreline (A) down to it (middle picture), in which case we read α as 0° 48.7' On the scale. Or we can use the shoreline as the horizon and bring the breakwater up to it by rotating the dial off the scale as in the right hand picture, in which case α reads 0° 53.5' Off the scale. The sum of these divided by two should be the right answer, eliminating the need for an IC measurement, as explained in the Appendix. This gives α = 0° 51.1' and d = 434 yd from the Table 11 calculator. However, the On sight seemed easier to align than the Off one, and so α = 48.7' On + 1.3' IC = 50.0' and this gives d = 442 yd. Either method is far more accurate than could be read from any chart, but a careful zooming on Google Earth image shows the distance is 449±2 yd. These sights were taken with a metal sextant. The lighting and geometry will more often than not favor one way over the other, as it did in this case. If we really wanted to know our very accurate location relative to this landmark, it would be best to use the horizontal methods of the next section. They can achieve this level of accuracy or better with a simple plastic sextant.*

Method 3 (horizon dip)

This measurement can be a trick play for racing sailors who want to know how far off a competitor is and they do not have radar. It will work whenever you can see a horizon beyond and above the target vessel. Then use a sextant to measure how far the waterline of the vessel (or islet) is below the horizon, and use Table 17 (or corresponding calculator) to find distance off. Again, for this one, which will have very small angles, you need an accurate IC and HE, and careful measurements.

Figure 3-5 shows an example of Method 3 to find distance to a breakwater. This method is so accurate that you could measure the distance to

the left of the green light and then to the right of the sign, to discover that the breakwater actually angles away from you at this perspective.

Method 3 works best from an elevated HE because that makes the angle bigger so percentage errors are now relatively smaller. You can, for example, stand on the boom, for a somewhat better result than standing in the cockpit.

A metal sextant with good scope will definitely give better results than plastic with Method 3. The results from Table 11 calculator are very sensitive to the angle and to the HE, which must be known to the foot.

This technique was invented in 1845 to be used by British war ships to determine the distance to a target vessel whose height they did not

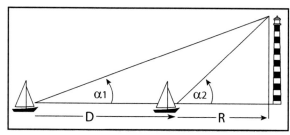

Figure 3-6. *Method 4. Taking two vertical angles to find distance off a landmark of unknown height. The procedure is equivalent to a running fix.*

know, so they could range in on it with their cannon fire. It was a clever solution and the inventor eventually became an admiral. There were, however, other ways to find distance off of a landmark or ship whose height was unknown. One such method was also published at about the same time, which we have reformulated and present as Method 4.

Method 4 (running fix, unknown H)

If we take a second Method-1 measurement after sailing a known distance toward a prominent landmark, we can then find distance off of this landmark without knowing its height. The answer is a result of basic trigonometry. The procedure is analogous to a standard running fix. If the landmark with unknown height is shown on the chart, we have a proper chartable fix; if we do not have a chart or the landmark is not shown, then this is a relative location.

Referring to Figure 3-6, measure α1 then travel a distance d toward the target and measure α2. Then compute the distance off the target

$$R = D \times \text{Tan}(\alpha 1) / [\text{Tan}(\alpha 2) - \text{Tan}(\alpha 1)] .$$

Figure 3-7 is a reminder of how to advance a circle of position (COP) for a running fix. This procedure applies to any of the methods used so far to find distance off. All we need for this is the course and distance run between the two angle measurements and the two ranges found from the two angle measurements. Plot the first COP,

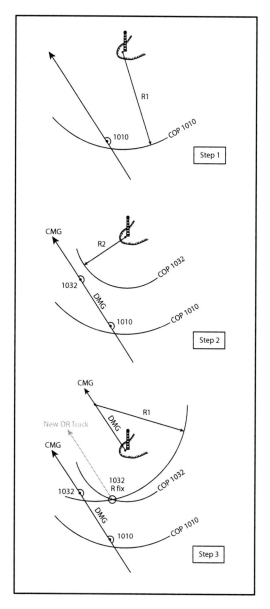

Figure 3-7. *Example of advancing a circle of position (COP). Step 1. A COP was measured at 1010, which shows the DR was off somewhat at the time. Step 2. After traveling a distance DMG along course CMG, a second COP was taken at 1032 and plotted. Step 3. Advance the center location of the COP by the course and distance made good between sights and draw the 1010 COP again. The intersection of this advanced COP and the second COP is your running fix (Rfix). Start a new DR track from the new Rfix.*

then plot the second COP, then advance the first to the second for the running fix. The accuracy of a running fix depends primarily on the accuracy of your DR between the two sights. If you change course between sights, then first figure the course and distance made good and use that to advance the circle.

Vertical danger angles

Vertical angles to landmarks of known elevation can also be used effectively for danger angles, to guard against getting too close to underwater hazards. The process has been described since the earliest writing on sextant piloting, and was championed by Lecky, who published a one-time popular book on that subject alone. We cover this topic in the later section on horizontal danger angles.

Horizontal Angles

So far we have discussed how an inexpensive plastic sextant can be used to find distance off of various landmarks. This can be for finding distances to land tens of miles away using the tip of a mountain peak on the horizon, or finding the distance to a nearby vessel just hundreds of yards away. These techniques each involved measuring a vertical angle, holding the sextant in its normal orientation.

These distance-off measurements provide a means of finding a position fix from a single landmark and in that sense contribute to the step from the "ordinary knowledge of seaman" to that of a navigator. Most basic fixes we learn require two identifiable landmarks, such as two crossed compass bearings or two (transit) ranges, or maybe a range and a depth contour. The step to finding position from a single body, such as doing a running fix from the only light showing through in the fog, is a key one to becoming a versatile navigator, and distance off by sextant adds another method to this category. The distance from a peak and the compass bearing to that same peak provides a position fix from just one landmark.

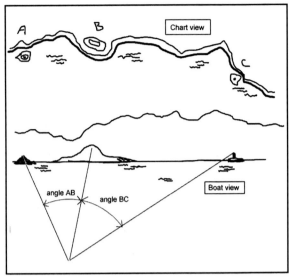

Figure 3-8. *Schematic view of three potential targets for a horizontal sextant angle fix, as they might appear from the boat and on a chart.*

Now we come to the real claim-to-fame of sextant piloting by turning the sextant sideways and measuring the horizontal angles between known landmarks on the horizon. From this we can find our position to remarkable accuracy—accurate enough to check the GPS in many circumstances. This procedure has attracted navigators and mathematicians since the very invention of the sextant in the mid 1700s. The procedure can be done with the simplest of plastic sextants or with your best ocean going instrument.

The horizontal angle between two landmarks on the horizon determines a unique circle of position on the chart (COP) that you must be located upon in order to observe that angle. As it is with a line of position (LOP) that you might get from a compass bearing to a lighthouse, you know you are on that circle, but you don't know where on the circle.

The procedure is to hold the sextant sideways, parallel to the ground, and measure the angle AB between two objects, A and B. For analogy to the vertical sights, one object serves as the horizon for the other. It is like taking a compass

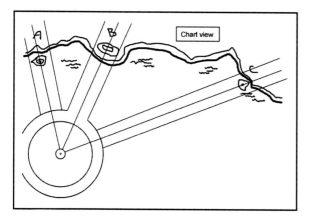

Figure 3-9. *Using a three-arm protractor to plot a horizontal sextant angle position fix. Set left arm to angle AB and set right arm to angle BC, then holding the angles fixed, slide the protractor around the chart till each arm crosses through its target and your position is in the center of the protractor which includes a small hole for a pencil mark. Without a three-arm protractor, the fix can be found graphically by plotting both circles of position.*

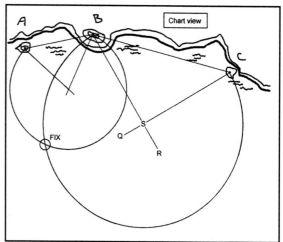

Figure 3-10. *Graphic solution to the three-body problem. There are numerous solutions. This is the easiest if we do not include numeric computations in the process. Plot procedure:*

1. *Draw line B-C*
2. *Construct angle CBR = 90°- angle BC*
3. *Construct Angle BCQ = 90°- angle BC*
4. *From intersection S, draw circle with radius SC*
5. *Vessel is on that circle*

Do the same with measured angle AB. The fix is the intersection of those two circles. A summary is in Fig 3-11 and an alternative method is shown in Fig 3-12.

bearing to each of them and then subtracting to get the angle between them, only now we do this very accurately. We are very lucky to get compass bearings accurate to ±2°, but with a sextant we can easily measure the angle to within ±0.02° (1.2′)—and with care, much better than that.

The crux of this method is how you plot that unique COP on the chart knowing the location of the two objects and the angle between them. There are several methods. The simplest, mentioned mostly to illustrate the principle, is use the compass rose to fold a piece of paper to the angle measured, then slide it around on the chart keeping one side on each object, marking a point at the apex of the triangle every so often. In doing so, you see clearly the principle behind the method, but this is not a very tidy solution. There is a special plotting tool, called a three-arm protractor (or station pointer), that makes this easier and more accurate—for this application, you only use two of the arms.

Without a three-arm protractor, you can plot the COP from a purely graphical solution as

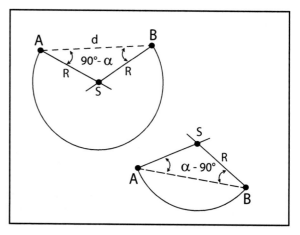

Figure 3-11. *Summary of the plotting procedure from Fig 3-10, including the case where a is greater than 90°. The angle α = Angle BC or Angle AB*

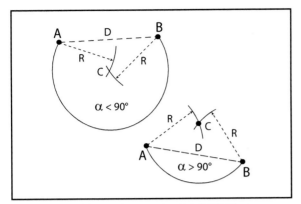

Figure 3-12. *Alternative way to plot COP. First compute R = D/[2sin(α)]. With a trig calculator at hand this is generally faster and more accurate than the pure graphic solution.*

shown in Figure 3-10, or use the compromise shown which combines a quick computation with a simple plot (Figure 3-11). One of these three methods is required to draw the COP on the chart—assuming you actually want the COP on the chart.

In a moment we look at reasons for drawing a COP on the chart, but if your goal is to get an actual fix, not just a COP, then you do not have to plot anything if you have the 3-arm protractor. Just take one more sight and then use a three-arm protractor for a quick and accurate fix, without drawing any lines at all. The process is illustrated in Figure 3-9 using 3 landmarks, A, B, and C, with angles A to B and B to C.

This type of fix can be used to check the GPS, or when anchored in a steep sided bay with no GPS, this is ideal for checking to see if you are dragging anchor.

It is a seemingly simple process, but there are subtleties involved. The engaging issue is that some configurations of landmarks offer better accuracy than others, and the challenge has been to make the best set of guidelines for the navigator to use in choosing the optimum targets. Lecky devoted a full chapter of 30 pages to this topic and the associated use of a station pointer. One of the last editions of Bowditch that includ-

ed guidelines for a good 3-body fix was the 1938 edition, which gives these criteria:

(a) When the center object of the three lies between the observer and a line joining the other two, or lies nearer than either of the other two

(b) When the sum of the right and left angles is equal to or greater than 180°

(c) When two of the objects are in range, or nearly so, and the angle to the third is not less than 30°

(d) When the three objects are in the same straight line

Transparency plotting

An attractive alternative to both the 3-arm protractor and the direct graphic method is the use of a transparent plotting sheet. In the old days, navigation stores and Navy supply offices issued transparent paper sheets with a large compass rose printed on them. With these you can plot the 2 angles (A to B, and B to C) and then just slide the transparency around over the chart to line up the lines and locate your fix. We illustrate this method in the next example.

The transparency method is essentially as fast as a 3-arm protractor, but sometimes even superior to the protractor in that it is easier to maneu-

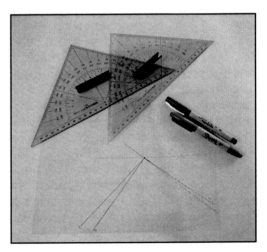

Figure 3-13. *Transparency plotting tools. It also works with tracing paper or vellum. See related Figure 3-14.*

ver once the lines are drawn, and also for small angles or close distances, the 3-arm plotter arms can sometimes get in their own way, meaning they block out part of the chart you need to see. This is never a problem with the transparency. The transparencies are also easier to store, and it is a nice way to practice this method before you obtain a 3-arm protractor (References).

There are multiple modern solutions. There is a durable draftsman's translucent paper called vellum that can take pencil lines and erasures on one side. These could be used with a rolling plotter or triangles to draw the lines, which would eventually be erased. You can use multiple places on the sheet for the center. Or you might scan a compass rose from a radar plotting sheet and print it on vellum at print shop.

Figure 3-13 shows the system we used for our next example, plotting with an ultra-fine sharpie on overhead transparency film. The "permanent" ink can be removed with alcohol, which brings to mind the famous navigator W.C. Fields, who said we should always carry a small bottle of alcohol in the chart table in case of snake bite—and, he added, we should also carry a small snake.

Vellum sheets can also be used in the nav station to advance depth contours for good fixes in the fog when other options might not be available. They are also a quick way to do a standard running fix of any kind without writing on the chart.

A way to practice 3-body fixes

The best approach is to just do it. And here is a wonderful way to practice right from home without having to go to the boat. Look around your neighborhood for three prominent landmarks (A,B,C) some distance off that span some reasonable spread of the horizon (see guidelines above). Then check that you can identify these target objects on the Google Earth (GE) image of your location. You can use edges of distant buildings or even telephone poles a block or two away. Google Earth's image view might help you locate good targets. Now use a sextant to measure the angles A to B and B to C. Print the im-

age from Google Earth as large as you can that shows all objects and where you were standing. This is your "chart." An example is given in Figure 3-14.

Then use the methods outlined above to find out where you were when you took the sights. This is an easy way to learn the nuances and beauties of the method very quickly. Books in the References go into more details of the process and analysis. It is an engaging navigation sport—and a good way to survey your local bay if you care to. We have an uncharted rock just barely awash in our local bay that kayakers and stand-up paddlers hit periodically at near-zero tide. With these techniques we could locate it precisely and put it on local charts till we have time to permanently mark it with a float.

Three-point fix example

Referring to Figure 3-14, standing at our front door, we took sights between three telephone poles, A, B, C, which we could locate on GE. Pole B base was under a tree, but could be located precisely relative to the curbs. We used a Davis Mark 3. It had an IC of 11' off. Corrected angles were:

Horizontal sextant angles in Fig. 3-14		
Position 1	AB	35° 37'
Position 1	BC	90° 53'
Position 2	AB	38° 11'
Position 2	BC	95° 47'

The position 2 sights were taken just 5 feet to the west—two side steps to the west. Notice how much the angles changed with just this step, which testifies to the sensitivity of the method. Note, too, that it illustrates the guideline to take closer targets rather than farther ones when you can. In this case we could have taken just 1 step and still clearly seen the difference between the two fixes.

The fix positions were found by drawing the angles on a transparency using the tools of Fig 3-13. For this type of close precision, with this

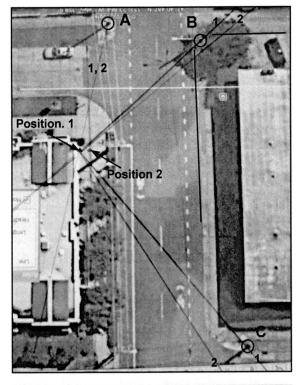

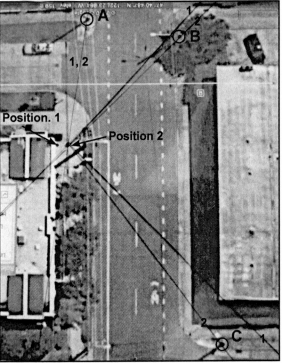

chart scale, the angles have to be plotted carefully and with a sharp pencil or ultra-fine ink tip.

After doing this a few times you develop the skill of locating all 3 points on the 3 lines: first 2, then add the last, and readjust the first 2. Then you can either punch a divider point through at the fix, or hold the transparency in place as you lift a corner to mark the fix.

This type of practice is best done with transparency or tracing paper. You can also practice the plotting method on a second printout to appreciate the value of the transparency method.

The vertical sextant angle methods described earlier are powerful tools, but they are not in the same league as the horizontal angle navigation illustrated here. Vertical angles are affected by uncertainty in horizons and in the location and elevations of the targets. Horizontal angle navigation, on the other hand, is often described as having an accuracy that is only limited by the accuracy of your charts.

Correcting for vessel motion

All methods described so far for both vertical and horizontal angles assume you are not moving during the fix or when drawing a COP. When moving, all sights become running fixes and we must account for the vessel motion for the most accurate results. Method 4 explained the running fix and how to advance a COP. This was used then as a technique to find distance off an object of unknown height, but that was actually a much more general procedure that can be applied to any range measurement that gives you a

Figure 3-14. *Google Earth view of a 3-point fix with a Mark 3 plastic sextant, taken outside of Starpath HQ, from two positions, separated by just 5 feet, and easily distinguished in this method. The base location of the top right telephone pole beneath tree cover could be located accurately relative to the line of the curbs. A circled dot has been drawn at each base point used. The measured angles were drawn on a transparency, and then fitted to the targets. The line to A as drawn on the transparency is common to both plots. For a reference scale, the GPS uncertainty in position would be wider than the width of the street.*

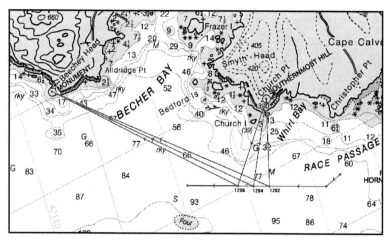

Figure 3-15. *Three sets of bearing lines and the corresponding horizontal angles that would yield COPs. The measurements are taken 2 minutes apart, traveling at 6 kts, or 0.20 nmi per leg.*

Time	Church Pt (CP)	Beechey Hd BH)	COP
1202	357	292	65°
1204	008	294	74°
1206	018	296	82°

COP, or to any two ranges taken from two different targets. These you could in principle take at the same time, using two observers, and then no running fix (rFix) is needed. But if one person is doing both sights, there will be some time spent between them that has to be accounted for. There are logical guidelines to follow in these cases, which might alleviate the need for the rFix.

A happy circumstance is when you might be sailing along a natural range (transit), meaning two charted landmarks are lined up, dead ahead. Then any COP that cuts this range is an instantaneous and very accurate fix with no further adjustment needed. Just record the time of the angle measurement, and that is the time of your fix. This is such a good way to navigate that you should always keep on the look out for this opportunity.

More commonly, you might be using two COPs for the fix from two different bodies. In cases like this we treat the two sights just as you would two compass bearings or two radar ranges. Take the one that is changing the most slowly first and then take the other one. In Figure 3-15, for example, suppose we are sailing west, south of Church Pt, one of our targets, with Beechey Head on the starboard bow being the other target. Compare the bearings shown in the table. If you erroneously crossed the 1202 CP bearing with the 1204 BH bearing, your fix would be off

by about 0.23 nmi, but if you crossed the 1202 BH line with the 1204 CP line, the error is reduced to 0.06 nmi, which is the improvement we get by taking first the one that changes least.

Or better still, take 1202 BH (slow one), then 1204 CP (fast one), then take 1206 BH again. Then plot the average of BH 1202 and 1206, with the 1204 CP and you get an accurate fix without any running fix plotting.

That is the same philosophy to keep in mind when measuring COPs directly—it is just easier to picture with the simple bearing lines. Notice that the 1204 COP between CP and BH (74°) can be well approximated by the average between the 1202 and 1206 sights (73.5°).

With practice the order of measurements and ways to average them become more automatic and can save the extra plotting needed to correct them. In *Fundamentals of Kayak Navigation*, we have shown that paddlers can calibrate marks on their paddles to be used at arm's length to measure horizontal angles, and pre-draw COPs for crucial areas on their charts for effective no hands navigation while underway.

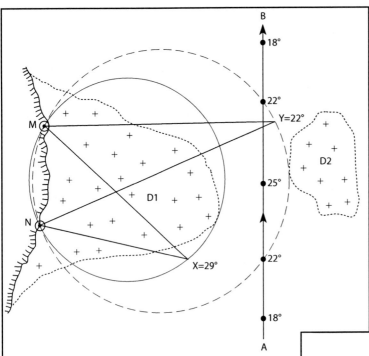

Figure 3-16. *Using the horizontal sextant angle between two landmarks, M and N, to guide you between two underwater hazards, D1 and D2, along course A to B. Everywhere on the solid circle the angle MN=29°; everywhere on the dashed circle, MN=22°. Once you cross over the MN=22° COP you want to be sure that the MN angle stays larger than 22° and smaller than 29°. The peak will be at about 25°. With someone to help, one person keeps M and N in view in the sextant at all times, calling out the angles, while another person steers. Picture adapted from a 1962* Bowditch.

Danger circles (horizontal)

You can use the COP itself to enhance a bearing fix by plotting the two compass bearings to A and B and then measure the angle A to B to get a COP. Choose your best fix as the point on the COP closest to the intersection of the two bearing lines. This is analogous to a standard technique of radar navigation using tangent bearings and a range.

Another application is to use a COP as a danger circle to keep you away from known dangers that you must pass in the presence of currents that could set you toward them. Once you find the sextant angle that marks your safe bearing, you monitor that angle as you pass and do not let yourself get set to a place where the angle reads larger than the danger angle. It is exactly analogous to using a danger bearing monitored by bearing compass, which is a common solution to this problem for those without radar. With radar, the variable range marker is usually the simplest and quickest solution to staying a

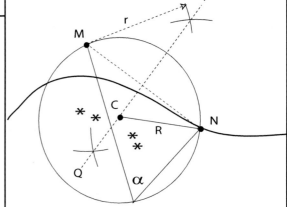

Figure 3-17. *To find the center of a danger circle based on two targets M and N we need to find the center of a circle that safely encompasses the danger and passes through both M and N. There are several solutions. One is draw the perpendicular bisector (PQ) of the line MN by swinging an arc or radius r from M and N, so they intersect as shown. The r can be any length greater than MN/2. Then with a drawing compass centered on the line PQ, move it till you find a location C with the radius CN that includes the danger. Another approach is choose any point on PQ to measure the desired angle, then find the center as explained in Figure 3-10.*

fixed distance off a good radar target. The well prepared navigator must have a deep bag of tricks to cover the varying circumstances that might occur, such as dangers off of a low flat beach that is not a good radar target.

The procedure is to find the sextant angle that makes a COP that encompasses the danger and then keep the sextant angle smaller (or larger) than that as you pass. As shown in the illustrations, this takes some plotting ahead of time, so this method is best done in preparation for a known hazard you must pass in the future. You can pre-draw several such COP segments on the chart to monitor your progress. In the example shown you would be hard pressed to solve that problem with danger bearings. You might want to use this method to back up your GPS anyway if you had to make this passage—we do still have the basic rule of good navigation that you should not rely on one aid alone if the matter is crucial.

Danger circles (vertical)

As noted in the vertical angles section, these danger angles can also be set up with vertical angles, and in many cases this might be easier or more convenient. For this, you need a prominent landmark whose elevation you know that will remain in view as you pass the danger. In some circumstances it could be crucial to account for the tides. Recall landmark elevations are relative to Mean High Water, which is not given in tide tables, but printed right on the charts. See *Lecky* for an extended discussion of this topic.

Taking Horizontal Sights

We have discussed the various things you can do with horizontal sextant sights, now we look at details of actually taking the sights.

The description is for using a traditional, split view horizon mirror. The full-view mirrors do not work well for horizontal angles in many circumstances, which is one of their disadvantages.

Sometimes these sights are better without a telescope and sometimes the telescope helps, but it's focus can be an important part of the adjustment in these landmark observations. Personal eyesight may enter into the telescope decision. Usually these sights can be made with eyeglasses on.

If you do not use a telescope, then this is the one place in sextant usage that a sextant sighting tube or "collimation tube" is useful. Without it, you can end up viewing your targets from the wrong angle which can prevent alignment or yield inaccurate results. The Davis Mark 3 has a built in one, and if you cut it off like we did in one model, then make a similar attachable version. The Mark 15 comes with one in the box.

Consider us looking at three targets on the horizon, called Left (L), Middle (M), and Right (R).

Step 1. Check the index correction and adjust if needed. For horizontal sights a measurement using the horizon or *distant* hilltop is plenty adequate in all cases. The most we would be off is

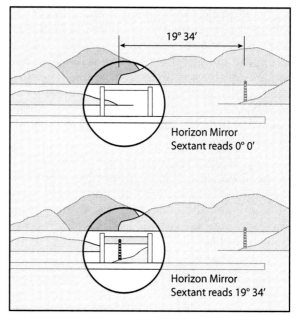

Figure 3-18. *View through a sighting tube on Mark 3 doing a horizon sight*

a minute or two and this will not affect any of these results. Celestial sights, of course, require the very best IC possible.

Step 2. Set sextant to 0° 0′, and hold it horizontal with the right hand, roughly parallel to the shoreline with the index and horizon mirrors facing up, and look straight toward the left target L. Orient the sextant so L appears in the glass or open space just above the center of the horizon mirror. If using a telescope make a check on the focus to see if optimized for your target.

If you lose orientation looking through the scope or sighting tube, then open the other eye! It is easy to forget this.

Step 3. With the left hand, slide the index arm away from you slowly, watching the shoreline in the mirror move to the right in the mirror. The idea here is to bring the center of the middle target M into view in the mirror just below the center of Left target. If using a telescope make a check on the focus to see if optimized for your new target.

Step 4. Unless you are lucky, the Middle target M will not appear in the mirror without a slight adjustment of the angle of the sextant relative to the horizon. That is, if you hold it perfectly parallel to the shoreline, you will not see M appear, but just the shoreline below it or terrain or sky above it. So the crucial step here is to rotate (roll) the sextant slightly till you see M or some part of the shoreline near M that informs you which way you have to go: more to the right or more to the left.

Step 5. Once you have them both in sight, L in the direct view, M in the mirror below it, carefully adjust the index arm until they are precisely lined up, and then read and record the sextant scale for your answer: the horizontal angle between L and M.

If there is any doubt about what the center points of your targets are and how they might appear on the chart, then double check that now if possible before the measurements are completed. Sometimes the target choice must be iterated, meaning look at the chart for a guess of good targets, then check the horizon, then back to the chart knowing what you can see to confirm your choice.

Step 6. Then do the same thing again, replacing L with M and M with R, to obtain the second answer: the horizontal angle between M and R.

Miscellaneous procedures

To complete our outline of this diverse topic of sextant piloting, we mention a few techniques implied in the earlier discussion. These are tools for the versatile navigator's bag of tricks. We confront continually changing conditions and perspectives on pilotage waters, so the more tools we have the better we are prepared.

Natural range and COP

Any two charted objects that line up from your perspective is called a range or transit. If you can identify these objects on the chart, you have one of the best possible lines of position. If you can then cross this LOP with a COP from a sextant angle (vertical or horizontal) you have a very precise fix, especially for the horizontal variety.

Two compass bearings and a COP

Crossed compass bearings is a common way to find a fix, but this fix can be greatly enhanced by adding a COP determined from the horizontal angle between them. Your position is then the location on the COP that is closest to the intersection of bearing lines. See Figure 3-19.

Depth contour and a COP

If the only navigation aids in view above the water can provide only a single COP (such as two landmarks too close together for a bearing fix) then a COP from them crossed with a depth contour is one way to get a position. This is not a strong fix in that depth contours have some uncertainty, even after correcting for tide and draft, but it could well be better than just a single bearing and a contour line.

It is a good exercise to compare compass bearing fixes with the intersection of two COPs.

Sextant as pelorus

A pelorus is a device to measure bearings relative to the bow of the boat. They are sometimes called a "dumb compass" or "azimuth ring." They are a double gimbaled compass card in a square box with cross-card sighting vanes to measure precise bearings. An edge of the box is aligned with the center line of the boat to establish the lubber line of the card at 000 R (relative), dead ahead. A pelorus sighting of a target on the starboard beam, could show that its actual bearing was 093 R. Then if we were holding a steady magnetic course of 200M, we would know the magnetic bearing of the target was 293M.

These instruments are common on steel vessels, where a conventional magnetic bearing compass would not be dependable. In fact, even on wood and fiberglass boats, these might yield more accurate bearings, because local magnetic disturbances occur on all vessels. Even on land you might get different compass bearings with your eyeglasses or watch off, compared to on.

A pelorus measurement from an aligned unit, can be used anywhere on the boat, which makes them convenient on powerboats where they can be used in comfort from the wheelhouse. They are standard equipment for predicted log racers, who are among the elite of precision inland navigators.

A good pelorus, however, is quite expensive, and these days hard to find. Davis Instruments made an economical model at one time that met basic needs, but it is no longer available. Luckily they still make the Mark 3 sextant, and that will do this job very nicely.

The horizontal sextant angle from the bow to a target on the horizon is just the relative bearing of that target that a pelorus would measure. These bearings can be used to find conventional compass bearing lines (relative to the steering compass), which in turn can be used for distance off by two bow angles and other techniques. It is another way to find distance from an *uncharted* landmark.

A common pelorus application is "swinging ship" to check the steering compass. In this method (see Reference books) you measure the relative bearing to a distant landmark of known magnetic bearing while steering a steady course on the cardinal and intercardinal compass headings. On near-shore waters without a distant landmark available, a navigational or natural range can be measured as you sail across it on the required compass headings.

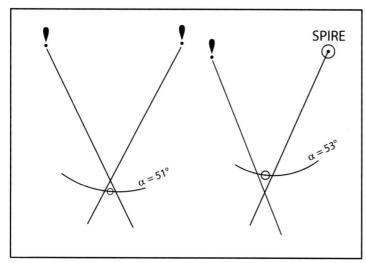

SPIRE

Figure 3-19. *Improving a compass bearing fix with a horizontal angle. On the left, the difference in compass bearings was 55°, but a quick sextant horizontal angle showed a separation of 51°, which pushed the fix back from the crossed LOPs. Likewise on the right, the bearings differed by 46°, when the true separation was 53°, which moves the fix closer to the targets. A sum of magnetic compass errors of this magnitude (4-6° or so) is not at all unexpected. Sextant angles just accurate to the degree are plenty good enough for this method, and these are quick and easy to take*

Summary

Sextant fixes are superior to compass bearing fixes because they are not susceptible to the several factors that limit bearing accuracy. Also they are always more accurate. In cases where the only targets are close together, bearing lines do not give good fixes, but the sextant angles still could do a very good job. When navigating narrow unmarked channels with the only landmarks a long way off, sextant piloting can keep you on course, whereas compass bearings would not be accurate enough.

On steel vessels, piloting by compass or gyrocompass requires the use of azimuth rings or gyro repeaters. This means that piloting can only take place from a specific location on the vessel. One of the reasons these methods have always been part of naval training is the sextant piloting can be done from any location on the vessel, which is a crucial asset if the standard nav stations have been compromised.

In 1829, the French hydrographer C.F. Beautemps-Beaupre said of sextant piloting:

> "We persist in believing that once navigators have made use of the method, they will renounce the use of compass bearings for fixing the position whenever they are navigating along coasts and they have good charts at their disposal."

It has not come about this way, but we strongly encourage practice with a simple Davis Mark 3 sextant and a 3-arm protractor to learn how such enthusiasm might have occurred, and to learn how it might fit into your routine means of backing up the GPS. Once learned, it will be surprising that this is not more used by contemporary navigators, both recreational and professional.

For those involved in GPS caching games, you should be able to stash a prize in a location relative to local landmarks in view using sextant piloting more accurately than you can with a GPS, which will often have uncertainties of ±50 ft or so. To convince yourself, do something like what we did in Figure 3-14. GPS is not even a close competitor to the sextant in this type of navigation. It might be interesting to check back through pirate lore and logbooks to see if we might find any hints to their having used this method for stashing treasure.

FURTHER READING AND RESOURCES

Books

Celestial Navigation—A Complete Home Study Course by David Burch, (Starpath Publications, 2009).

A Complete Epitome of Practical Navigation by J.W. Norie (J. W. Norie & Co., 12th ed. 1839).

Davis Masters Sextants User's Guide, 00026.710, Rev. F (Davis Instruments, 2008).

The Ebbco Sextant—Is Use, Care, and Adjustment by J.G.P. Weatherlake, (Higgs Group, 1960s). The original manual. Online

Emergency Navigation by David Burch (McGraw Hill, 2nd edition, 2009)

Fundamentals of Kayak Navigation by David Burch (Globe Pequot Press, 4th edition, 2008)

A History of the Navigator's Sextant by Charles H. Cotter, (Brown, Son & Ferguson, 1983).

How to Find your Position with a Sextant by William A. Davis (Davis Instruments, 1966, 1968). The original Davis manual, second edition said *"...with a Master Sextant"* and was with co-author Stephen M. Russell

Inland and Coastal Navigation by David Burch (Starpath Publications, 2009).

Lifeboat Sextant—Instructions for Use in Finding Latitude and Longitude Together with Simple Sailing Instructions by W. J. Eckert (U.S. Naval Observatory, 1944). We believe this is the original manual for the US Navy plastic sextant (Culver 1940).

Long Term Almanac, Sun and Stars, 2000-2050 by Geoffrey Kolbe, (Starpath Publications, 2009). Includes sight reduction tables to make it a one-book celestial navigation solution.

A Manual of Spherical and Practical Astronomy. Vol II. Theory and Use of Astronomical Instruments by William Chauvenet (J.B. Lippincott & Co, 1863) The sextant is covered in Chapter IV.

The Nautical Sextant by W. J. Morris (Paradise Cay, 2010). Detailed, well illustrated descriptions of sextant workings of models from 1850 to modern times.

The Sextant by H. Wilburforce Clarke, (W. H. Allen & Co, 1885).

The Sextant and its Applications—Including the Correction of Observations for Instrumental Errors, and the Determination of Latitude, Time, and Longitude by Various Methods on Land and at Sea, with Examples and Tables by W,H. Simms (Troughton and Simms, 1858).

The Sextant Handbook by Bruce Bauer (McGraw Hill, 2nd edition, 1992)

The Sextant and Other Reflecting Mathematical Instruments—with Practical Hints, Suggestions and Wrinkles, on their Errors, Adjustments and Use by F.R. Brainard (Van Nostrand, 1891)

Stark Tables for Clearing the Lunar Distance—and Finding Universal Time by Sextant Observation, including a Convenient Way to Sharpen Celestial Navigation Skills while on Land by Bruce Stark (Starpath Publications, 2010). A long tested method to find longitude without time that does not depend on computer solutions.

Taking the Stars by Peter Ifland, (Krieger Publishing Company, 1998). Beautiful pictures of older instruments and their history.

Wrinkles in Practical Navigation by S. T. S. Lecky (Geo Philip & Sons, 22nd edition, 1947). Online in full in various editions from 1881.

Articles

"A Recommendation of Hadley's Quadrant for Surveying, Especially the Surveying of Harbours, together with a Particular Application of it to some cases of Pilotage" by Rev. John Michell, B.D., F.R.S. (Philosophical Transactions, 1683-1775, p70. 1765)

"Precision Celestial Navigation Experiments" by Capt. Henry H. Shufeldt, USNR, The Journal of Navigation (RIN), Vol 15, p 301, 1962.

"Finding Distance—Not Knowing Height" by Peter Ifland, The Journal of Navigation (RIN), Vol 55, p294, 2002

Resources

Baader AstroSolar Safety Film. www.baader-planetarium.com. There are several US outlets including: www.astro-physics.com and www.scopecity.com. Purchased films should arrive with detailed instructions and cautions for its handling and applications. If not, contact the seller or see the Baader web site.

www.starpath.com/navpubs. A source for Bowditch sextant piloting tables and their related calculators, as well as other resources of interest to navigators.

www.ion.org/museum. Details of a US Navy station pointer at the Institute of Navigation's Virtual Museum can be found here under Marine/Map Plotting tools. The presentation was prepared and donated by Starpath.

www.historicalatlas.com/lunars. This web site was developed and is maintained by navigation historian Frank Reed. It provides a way to clear lunar distance measurements as well as predict the distances, which is a big aid to planning and taking the sights. A history of the subject is included.

www.staff.science.uu.nl/~wepst101/ldtab.html. A convenient source of precomputed lunar distances including much background on the subject by Steven Wepster.

APPENDIX

Contents

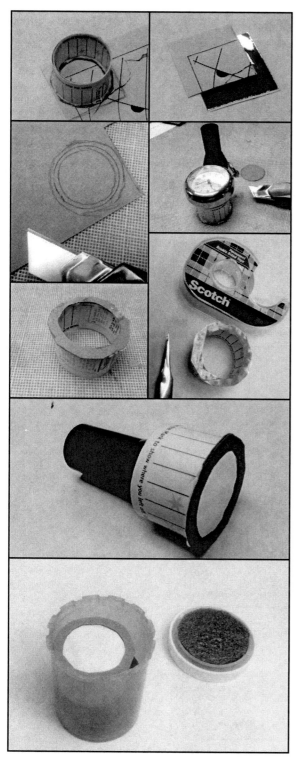

Construction of Baader Solar Filter

Check your sextant-telescope geometry first so you know how much room you have. Generally the filter tube assembly must be made fairly thin to allow the index arm to move past it without hitting it.

Step 1. Wrap several strips of thin cardboard around the telescope, to form a small tube about 1″ tall that just fits on your telescope. Glue these layers together to make the tube.

Step 2. With the Baader foil between two thin cardboard or paper sheets mark the size of piece that will be needed to cover the tube and cut this out.

Step 3. Make two cardboard base plate rings that have inside and outside diameters just a few mm smaller and bigger than the diameter of your tube.

Step 4. Glue the tube to the center of one of the rings. Here we show a pocket watch being used as a weight as this glue dries. We used Gorilla glue, that dries white in 15 min or so.

Step 4. Put a trimmed layer of double-sided adhesive tape on the top of the ring. This will be used to hold the foil on the end.

Step 5. Carefully place this adhesive side down onto the foil to stick it to the ring, then add the second ring on top of that using the same adhesive tape to protect the edges of the foil. Small wrinkles in the foil will not matter, but you can usually do this with very few wrinkles.

Step 6. Trim the edges of the rim as much as you can, and be sure that at least one orientation of the filter will allow the index arm to pass below it.

Step 7. Look for some fortuitous container that can serve for storage and protection. We found a plastic pill jar just right for this one, with a few pieces of foam inserted to hold it in place.

Figure A-1. *Steps in making a Baader Solar Filter for sextant telescopes.*

The Solar IC Method

This is a way—also called "On and Off Limb Method"—to get accurate IC measurements for cel nav sights and also a way to get small vertical angles more accurate with plastic sextants as it eliminates the IC from the measurement. Figure A-2 shows the procedure. We end up with two values of H read from the sextant, on the scale (H_{on}) and off the scale (H_{off}). Then we can combine these to get what we want:

$H_{on} = 2SD + IC$ and $H_{off} = 2SD - IC$.

Subtract the two equations to get:

$H_{on} - H_{off} = 2SD + IC - (2SD - IC) = 2\ IC$

so

$$(H_{on} - H_{off}) / 2 = IC.$$

Likewise,

$H_{on} + H_{off} = 2SD + IC + (2SD - IC) = 2 \times 2SD,$

so

$$(H_{on} + H_{off}) / 4 = SD.$$

When using this for vertical angle measurements, we would have $2SD = \alpha$ (the true angular height we want) so,

$$(H_{on} + H_{off}) / 2 = \alpha$$

Remember the H_{off} value needed here is 60.0′ minus what we actually read on the dial once alignment has been achieved.

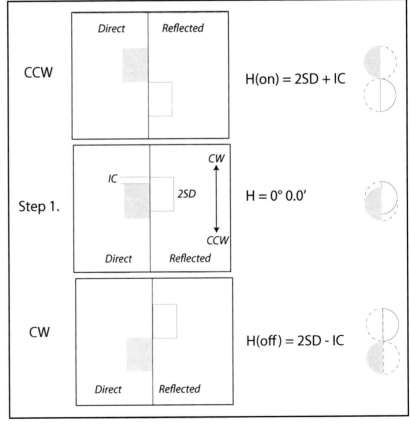

Figure A-2. The solar IC method. With sextant set to 0° 0.0' (Step 1) we view a distant building or mountain whose true angular height is "2SD." The direct and reflected images do not line up by precisely the Index Correction (IC) we want to measure. Recalling the jingle "If it is too high, it is too low" we know that turning the dial CCW (Away) will bring the Reflected image down, as the dial reading increases. Thus when we align the objects as in the top picture we will be On the scale. The amount we have to turn it is first the IC amount to get them even, then the 2SD amount to line up top of the right with bottom of the left. This will be a total dial turn of 2SD+IC.

Had we turned the other way, CW, the reflected image would rise in the view, and we would only need to turn 2SD-IC to align as shown in the bottom picture. These notes assume CCW is the direction of increasing sextant angle reading.

Plastic vs. Metal Sextant Results

A summary of this section is presented earlier in Part 2.

We did sun and moon sights underway and on land using metal and plastic sextants. Each of the average intercepts listed in the table of averages below represent 4 or more sights. The sun-moon sights were used for running fixes. Details are given below. No special analysis (such as slope fitting) was applied. The averages include all sights taken. All can be improved with more careful analysis.

These are the intercepts based on computer computations from the known GPS position at the time of the sights, and in that sense is a measure of the quality of the sights. Details of each sight session follow the table of results.

Set	Summary of averages	
1.	Metal underway moon	0.9' T ± 1.7
1a.	Metal underway sun	0.1' A ± 1.3
4.	Metal underway sun	1.6' T ± 0.4
6.	Metal on land sun	0.5' A ± 0.6
2.	Mark 15 underway sun	6.7' A ± 1.4
2a.	Mark 15 underway moon	4.3' A ± 1.4
5.	Mark 15 underway sun	5.1' A ± 1.0
3.	Mark 3 underway moon	8.4' T ± 2.5
3a.	Mark 3 underway sun	5.8' T ± 2.5
7.	Mark 15 on land sun	4.0' A ± 2.3
8.	Mark 3 on land sun	1.6' T ± 1.6

Data format notes

We use here a common navigation calculator input format for all angles, since that is the way we did the sight reductions, i.e. Lat 48° 25.6 N = 48.256, and Lon 125° 55.9'W = -125.559 (west is minus, east is positive). For sextant angles, Hs = 33° 02.5' = 33.025, etc. Times are likewise represented as decimals. 13h 23m 44s = 13.2344.

If a time has no seconds it is 12.45. We need to be clear on the zones, however, as several were used.

Sights underway

The route was Victoria, BC to Maui HI, on a Beneteau 455f sailboat during a yacht race. We were a crew of 8. Sights were all taken by the author under spinnaker in trade wind conditions, that is surfing in 8 to 10 foot seas with speeds varying from 7 to 14 kts and headings varying some ±20° or so—not ideal conditions for celestial sights, but still doable, which is one of the points we wanted to make with these data. The motivation for doing them at this particular time was an article in Cruising World that raised the issue of cel nav accuracy in general, on land vs. underway, etc. Indeed, one set of sights (first listed below) was taken standing at the boom, directly in the "line of battle"—that is, standing halfway between a food fight from the bow to the cockpit, which occurs in the normal course of events on a racing yacht once a case of spoiled bread rolls is discovered. This involved some dodging of the missiles and the occasional crash of a bread roll on the side of the sextant. Again, not ideal conditions for precision work, but at least not boring, even a bonus for the present study of environmental effects on sextant accuracy.

Log of positions for Sextant Sights			
PDT	GPS positions	CMG	SMG
15.44	32.067, -142.246		
17.06	31.594, -142.259	186 T	8.2 kts
17.19	31.555, -142.262	188 T	8.9 kts
17.54	31.489, -142.262	187 T	8.1 kts

At 15.44 PDT on July 5, 2000 our GPS position was 32.067, -142.246. At that time, the indicated SOG was 8.5 kts, and the COG was 185 T. Above we show the averages made good for several intervals that span the sights. Air temperature was 80° F, pressure was 1028 mb. The sun

was bright and very hot. Height of eye was estimated to be 11 feet (standing on the cabin top, heeled over more often than not), watch error was 4 s slow. All sights reduced by a navigation calculator.

For an assumed position (AP) to use for the sight reduction, we will just DR from the 15.44 position using average values made good to a later accurate position recorded at 17.06 of 31.555, -142.255. At this time recent values of SOG, COG were about 8.5 kts at 185 T, about the same as when we started. Unfortunately, these are the only two real positions we recorded in this interval. These two times and positions yield a CMG of 186 T and an SMG of 8.2 kts. Now we choose (arbitrarily, since it doesn't really matter which we use) 16.20 as the "sight time" and our DR position at this time was 32.018, -142.252.

Set 1. Metal sextant

IC = 0.0 (From 4 measurements taken after the sights using the horizon: 0.2' On, 0.0, 0.0, 0.0.) This sextant historically had 0.0 for IC, checked several ways on land over the past year or more, although in subsequent measurements taken a week later on land in Maui I got 1.0' On as the average of a long series of measurements! I never did figure out the explanation of the latter result. It was applied to the land sights but not to those underway. Both were horizon sights. Sometimes refraction can affect these things as well as psychological effects having to do with the actual colors of sky and ocean, relative brightness, etc.

The sextant used was a 15-year-old forerunner of the present day Astra 3b from China. Newer models turned out to be much nicer, but this one has served us well over the years. First intercepts are for S=0 and constant DR = 16.20 position, second set are advanced to actual sight times using 8.2 kts at 186T.

Set 1. Upper limb of the moon (16.20 DR)			
WT (PDT)	Hs	a -value (16.20 DR)	a -value
16.1220	51.115	1.0' A 115.7	0.6' A 115.7
16.1420	51.370	2.4' T 116.2	2.6' T 116.2
16.1533	51.490	1.0' T 116.5	1.2' T 116.5
16.1710	52.060	0.2' T 116.9	0.4' T 116.9
		Average =	0.9' T ± 1.7

Set 1a. Lower limb of the sun			
WT (PDT)	Hs	a -value (16.20 DR)	a -value
16.1954	64.396	1.2' T 254.8	1.2' T 254.8
16.2114	64.224	0.3' T 255.1	0.3' T 255.1
16.2222	64.072	0.9 A 255.4	1.0' A 255.4
16.2350	63.494	0.7' A 255.8	0.8' A 255.8
		Average =	0.1' A ± 1.3

If we assume the DR is correct (not guaranteed, of course, in our conditions) then the second set of intercepts is a measure of our accuracy. The average of the moon sights is 3.6/4 = 0.9' T. The average of the sun lines is -0.3/4 = 0.1' A. The spread is about ± 1' in each case, but we can later do better by a careful slope analysis of this data. In the meantime, the running fix obtained at 16.20 using all the data is off the DR position by 1.3 miles. Since our DR was likely uncertain by 0.5 mi or so, this is not bad. The sights could be improved with slope analysis (not done) to sort out which of the sights were best—or maybe it will get worse; we never know till we do it. It is a good sign that the sights are a mixture of Toward and Away a-values, which gives hope that the errors are more random than systematic.

Set 2. Mark 15 plastic sextant

The main issue with plastic sextant sights is the IC. The IC for the sun sights is taken to be 1.6' On the scale ± 2.4' as explained in the notes below. For these we will just update the DR using the logbook data above for each sight (15.44

to 17.06 for the sun lines, and 17.19 to 17.54 for the moon lines). Temp, Press, WE, HE are the same as Set 1. DR updated at each sight.

Set 2. Lower limb of the sun		
WT (PDT)	Hs	a -value
16.3600	61.152	6.3' A 258.6
16.3655	61.020	8.1' A 258.8
16.3743	60.540	6.2' A 258.9
16.3837	60.420	7.0' A 259.1
16.3917	60.350	5.7' A 259.2
Average =		6.7' A ± 1.4'

Then we ran for about an hour doing sights with other sextants, and resting from the heat of the sun. Then returned to the Mark 15. We will use these two sets of Mark 15 sights for a running fix. For the moon sights IC = 3.1' On the scale ±1.0'. See IC notes below.

Set 2a. Upper limb of the moon		
WT (PDT)	Hs	a -value
17.2557	63.153	4.6' A 139.9
17.2853	63.372	5.7' A 141.2
17.3001	63.488	2.9' A 141.7
17.3150	64.015	4.0' A 142.5
Average =		4.3' A ± 1.4'

The spread is not at all bad for a plastic sextant: 6.7' A ± 1.4' for the sun and 4.3' A ± 1.4' for the moon, but it is disconcerting that all sights are in the same direction, i.e. Away. This is almost certain proof that there is some systematic error in the data. Note that if the intercept (a) is Away = Hc - Ho, then Hs is too small, which means the 2 or 3' we took off in the IC was too much—or simply the sights are all just too low by that amount. For example, in the last sight if the IC was not -3 but +1 (ie 1' Off) then the a-value would have been about 0. The 17.30

fix obtained using all sights is 10.2 miles off of our 17.30 DR. This is a rather poor fix, but we do not have good IC data and the sights themselves were not taken in the proper manner as discussed in Part 2.

It is fair, however, to say that the sights themselves were only in error by 4.3 miles in one case and 6.7 miles on average in the other, and to stress that the error was in the same direction. This combination of LOPs gives a larger error in the two-body fix, but, with a well chosen set of 3 stars, near 120° apart, this near constant error would indeed cancel in large part, and yield a reasonably accurate fix. This is why it is so important to use star sights for fixes, not just running fixes with the sun. Even adding the moon does not help this.

It is interesting that the average a-values differed by 6.7 - 4.3 = 2.4, which is very roughly the same as the difference in IC's used (3.1- 1.6 = 1.5). In other words, the moon sights would have been 2 miles better using the sun line ICs. But all this is pure speculation, we simply have no better data at present. Later we will do the slope analysis to see if that helps, but we are rather out of range of those corrections.

Notes on the Set 2 index corrections

The index corrections were measured several times, but unfortunately not following the careful procedure described in Part 1. They were just taken in the Toward and Away (up and down) directions before and after each set of sights. Notation: "A3.2 On" means the IC was measured turning the micrometer drum in the Away direction and the value was 3.2' On the scale. Refer back to Part 1 to see how to do these properly.

Before the sun sights (16.32) we have 5 IC measurements	
A 4.2 On	T 0.5 On
A 4.0 On	T 1.5 On
A 3.2 On	
After the sun sights (16.40) we have 7 IC measurements	
A 2.2 On	T 2.5 On
A 0.0 On	T 2.0 On
A 0.0 On	T 1.0 Off
	T 0.0 On

Since these were not done with the "touch and leave" procedure and the sights themselves were not taken with the "set and wait" procedure, we do not have such nice results to work with. So for now we just do some averaging and note our uncertainty. The average of all 12 is 1.6′ On . The average of all 12 minus the highest (4.2 On) and the lowest (1.0 Off) is also 1.6′ On. For now let us just say the IC = -1.6′ and the uncertainty is ± 2.4′ for all the sun sights.

Before the moon sights (17.22) we have 4 IC measurements	
T 4.0′ On	A 4.0′ On
T 4.0′ On	A 4.5′ On
And after the moon sights (17.33) we have 4 IC again	
T 1.0′ On	A 3.0′ On
T 1.5′ On	A 3.0′ On

Here the average before the sights was 4.1′ On and the average after the sights was 2.1′ On. For now we will just say that for all moon sights IC = -3.1′ and the uncertainty is ± 1.0′ Again, we might do better with a more systematic approach but even with this data we are near the limit of plastic sextant accuracy so there is little justification for it. (At the date of these sights we did not appreciate the value of doing all sights Away, considering the two directions equal. But since we averaged the IC it is likely a reasonable result, just not optimized.)

Set 3. Mark 3 plastic sextant

This was a standard Mark 3, again a very old one, but with no telescope.

Notes on Set 3 index corrections

For the sun sights we set the IC to zero before each sight and then immediately proceeded to take the sight without further tests of this setting. During the subsequent moon sights and then later on land in Maui, I discovered that whenever I set it to 0 by eye and then measured it I would get 6′ Off the scale. This result was rather surprisingly consistent and reproducible—which only goes to show that the use of plastic sextants takes time and study. You must learn your "personal errors," a term described in Bowditch and elsewhere regarding sextant sights. When we did use this type of sextant in class in the early 80's, we would set them to zero (after a lot of tapping), then paint the adjustment screw threads with fingernail polish so they could not turn. It seemed to work well, so we never did do any systematic studies.

These days we find that the best IC measurement for plastic sextants is the solar method using a custom solar filter, and always in the Away direction. We did not have that experience at the time of this data, which we keep and present nevertheless because it shows the results doing the sights in the common manner. It is also the only documented metal-plastic comparison at sea that we have.

For now we have this large uncertainty floating around, but it turns out to not make that much difference: first we reduced with 0 for sun lines and +6 for the moon lines, then repeated with + 3 for all sights and got the same answer.

Set 3. Lower limb of the sun (DR updated at each sight, IC = 0)		
WT (PDT)	Hs	a -value
16.5047	58.18	2.7' T 261.5
16.5419	57.38	7.1' T 262.2
16.5643	57.06	5.3' T 262.6
17.0027	56.22	8.3' T 263.2
Average =		5.8' T ± 2.5

Set 3a. Upper limb of the moon (DR updated at each sight, IC = +6)		
WT (PDT)	Hs	a -value
17.4106	65.10	7.3' T 147.0
17.4147	65.16	6.2' T 147.5
17.4420	65.35	10.9' T 148.6
17.4750	65.54	8.0' T 150.5
17.4853	66.02	9.7' T 151.0
Average =		8.4' T ± 2.5

These sights all together give a 17.45 running fix which is 13 miles off the DR at that time. A slope analysis could improve this if it showed that the lower sights were better. Note an intercept labeled T, means the Ho were too big, which most likely means the +6 IC was too big. If we had used 0 as in the sun lines, each of these moon lines would be 6' lower and the fix much improved. Unfortunately, we did not have enough time to experiment with this underway.

In short, we did not do very well with these sights, but since all a-values are Toward (T) it implies there is definitely some systematic error (such as IC), or the instrument is just off that amount. Note from the plots that the scatter in the sunlines was also larger than with the moon lines which is what we also got with the other plastic sextant. There was a bright glare on the horizon from the sun during both of these sets so that might have contributed to this.

Set 4. Metal sextant underway

Set 4. PDT 7/9/00 GPS positions (same sextant as before)		
11.37	24.141, -151.290	
11.50	24.126, -151.304	CMG = 221 T, SMG = 9.1
12.11	24.106, -151.327	CMG = 226 T, SMG = 8.3

T = 80, P = 1030, HE = 11, IC=0, WE = 5s Slow. The notebook states VERY HOT with much glare, and my old sextant did not have good horizon shade options (the new models have this corrected) so sights were done without horizon shades with consequently not a very good horizon.

Set 4. Lower limb of the sun		
WT (PDT)	Hs	a -value (DR updated to each sight)
11.4046	41.450	1.5' T 081.1
11.4231	42.084	1.5' T 081.3
11.4359	42.264	0.1' A 081.4
11.4544	42.518	1.8' T 081.5
Average =		1.6' T ± 0.4 or so...

The results are not too bad for the conditions, poor horizon and surfing in big seas. The positions used for comparisons cannot be too poor, however, since we only ran for 2 miles during the sights. Here we really must consider the "best sight' (0.1') as an anomaly and more likely the average with the poor horizon was more like 1.6'.

Set 5. Plastic Mk 15 sextant underway

Again, I did not do proper "touch and leave" IC measurements, so the data are not as good as they could be. Also the sights themselves were not taken in the "set and wait" procedure, so we don't know which to use anyway.

Before sights at 11:56		After sights at 12:05	
T 3.0 On	A 7.0 On	T 5.0 On	A 8.0 On
T 3.0 On	A 6.5 On	T 5.0 On	A 7.0 On
		T 5.0 On	A 6.0 On

Hence we will just average all of them and use: 55.5/10 = 5.5′ ± 3 On the scale for all sights. In principle we could do better if we followed the methods of Section 1. HE, WE, T, P same as in Set 4. DR using logbook of Set 4.

Set 5. Lower limb of the sun		
WT (PDT)	Hs	a -value (DR updated to each sight)
11.5846	45.460	4.4′ A 082.4
11.5846	45.460	4.4′ A 082.4
12.0100	46.154	5.1′ A 082.5
12.0443	47.044	6.1′ A 082.8
Average =		5.1′ A ± 1.0

Again, the spread is not bad, but we are fighting an unknown IC in this case with an uncertainty of 3 miles. But we can at least say that the sights are accurate to within about 5 miles *without any sophisticated analysis at all*, which is one of the points we wanted to make. And these are underway, in poor but realistic conditions; not on land.

Set 5. Metal sextant underway

Set 5. PDT 7/20/00 GPS positions (same sextant as before)		
16.04	37.280, -133.574	
16.47	37.233, -134.028	CMG = 222 T, SMG = 9.0

All data same as earlier sights but WE = 3s Slow, Temp = 70°F, Pressure = 1030 mb.

Lower limb of the sun		
WT (PDT)	Hs	a -value (DR updated to each sight)
16.3236	54.080	0.2′ A 257.1
16.3404	53.521	0.8′ T 257.4
16.3527	53.356	0.2′ T 257.7
16.3748	53.100	1.7′ T 258.2
16.3943	52.484	2.2′ T 258.6
Average =		0.9′ T ± 1.0

In this set, it looks like the last two are two big, but a slope analysis of this data does not discern any of the 5 as being outside of the error bars, which is a good lesson in not discarding data without a careful slope analysis. Again, in any event, one can conclude that the cel nav LOP was right to within 1 mile.

Set 6. Metal sextant on land

Overlooking the beach on Maui at 20.5753, -156.4110. July 12, 2000. Very hot. Shade temp = air temp = 85° F, but leaving the thermometer in the sun it heated to 111° F in about 20 minutes. In short, if a plastic sextant is going to go weird in the sun, now will be its time! HE = 17 feet (measured to the foot). Sight times in HST (ZD = +10). WE = 6s Slow. Pressure was 1018 mb.

As mentioned earlier, I found an unusual IC for these sights on land since this sextant has usually had a 0.0 correction. The data were (all On the scale): 1.5, 1.0, 1.2, 1.0, 0.8, 1.0, for an average of 1.0′ On the scale, which is what we use here.

WT (HST)	Hs	a -value (from true position)
17.4149	18.401	0.5' A 286.8
17.5323	16.060	0.3' A 287.6
17.5509	15.426	0.2' A 287.7
18.2131	9.537	1.0' A 289.6
18.2256	9.362	0.0' T 289.7
18.2406	9.196	1.4' A 289.8
Average of all =		0.5' A ± 0.6

This one is difficult to analyze as the data covers such a large Hs change. It is always best to take at least 4 sights each in a sequence for a better slope analysis. It is hard to do slope analysis over such a large gap. However, since the first and second group differ so much, chances are that a careful analysis of each independently might improve this result—but it won't be too much since we are already well below 1.0' accuracy.

Set 7. Mark 15 plastic sextant on land

Note on IC: Unfortunately, again, a careful job in this was not done, but it was these measurements that in part led to the formulation of proper procedures presented in Part 1.

Here are the recorded data:

Time	Toward	Away	Comment
17.45	T 4.0 On	A 1.0 Off	just after first sight
17.56	T 1.0 Off	A 0.0	just before 2nd sight
	T 1.0 On		
18.04	T 0.5 On	A 5.0 Off	after last sights
	T 0.5 On	A 5.0 Off	

For now, we just average all of these and use that and note the uncertainty. We get 6 On and 12 Off = 6 0ff / 9 = 0.7' Off with an uncertainty of ± about 4'. One can do better as we will show later on doing more sights with good proce-

dures. For now: IC = 0.7' Off for all sights. Else, same data as in Set 6.

WT (HST)	Hs	a -value (DR = actual position = constant)
17.4435	17.556	6.3' A 287.0
17.5850	14.472	4.9' A 288.0
18.0040	14.244	3.4' A 288.1
18.0251	13.574	1.5' A 288.3
Average =		4.0' A ± 2.3'

Note that not only is there clearly some systematic error, i.e. all are Away, but there is also a trend, the a-values getting smaller, in this case it is towards better sights, but that is not significant. The bigger worry is that it does seem to be changing. Slope analysis might not help much with clearly systematic errors. It is definitely possible that this sextant was not in equilibrium with the local temperature, which was extremely hot. In any event, for now, we concentrate on the value itself, 4 miles, which is not bad for a plastic sextant, even without special care and in the burning sun!

Set 8. Mark 3 plastic sextant on land

The measured IC of the instrument was 6' Off the scale. It was this before the sights and after and it is the same as it was underway. Also as mentioned earlier, I can take this one and twiddle the mirrors and then reset them to what appears to be zero when viewing the horizon, and then twiddle the index arm and measure the IC and get 6' Off again. This is a bit surprising, but we will live with it. Take our small blessings as they come. We call the IC 6' Off the scale. Else data are the same as in Set 6 and 7. Recall this sextant can only be read to a precision of 2' and that requires the use of a vernier scale.

WT (PDT)	Hs	a -value (DR = actual position = constant)
17.5057	16.34	2.4' T 287.4
18.1313	11.40	3.3' T 289.0
18.1419	11.24	1.8' T 289.1
18.1633	10.54	1.2' T 289.3
18.1757	10.34	0.5' A 289.4
Average =		1.6' T ± 1.6

This of course is excellent, and must be considered part luck. One should consider a consistent under 10 miles as good for this device. On the other hand, it is not surprising to us to see the Mark 3 do as well as the Mark 15. We have noticed this in the past. I am not sure it will hold up if we use optimum procedures with the Mark 15. Part of the reason is you must always move the index arm of the Mark 3 in the same direction. At least with my operation of it, the only way I can very carefully squeeze and push it to a new angle is to push it down. So if I am below the angle, I must crudely set it too high and then carefully push it down. In other words, the very simple design of the instrument forces users to operate it in a consistent way. And—most important—this is the same motion needed to check the IC, so both are done in the same manner. Also, since there are no optics and the arm is so difficult to set carefully, one is forced to use the "set and wait" method, which is the best way to do plastic sextant sights.

Conclusion

Hopefully we have made our point about plastic sextant sights. It has taken a lot of time to document what we and many others knew was true without these most elementary examples. There are also numerous accounts elsewhere, both documented and anecdotal that support the conclusion that a plastic sextant can get consistent fixes within 5 or 6 miles by averaging multiple sights, even if each of the sights themselves may be off by this amount or even more.

Our recent work with plastic sextant lunars and solar IC method using Baader filters, encourages us to propose that with care you can do even notably better than that.

There are more examples of these comparisons in the Testimonials section below.

Footnotes

1. Temperature dependence of IC

There is a published study that showed a large temperature dependence of the index correction of Davis plastic sextants, but it is not at all clear that this study is pertinent to practical navigation—nor that the author actually did measure what he set out to. See: "Temperature Dependence of Index Error," R. Egler, Navigation, Journal of the Institute of Navigation, 42, No.3, Fall 1995. That experiment should be repeated in more realistic circumstances before its conclusions can be extended to real navigation underway. Several important matters of plastic sextant usage were not mentioned.

2. Optimizing sextant sights

Optimizing sextant sights is discussed in Bowditch section 1609 of recent editions. Unfortunately this is a shortened presentation compared to earlier versions and sadly omits the slope fitting method. Check section 1507 of 1977 or earlier editions, which discuss this most important technique. They may have discontinued the discussion because they had used *Pub 214* to compute the slope and that pub went out of print at that time. But you can obviously compute the slope with any sight reduction method.

3. Ebbco history

The "Ebbco" name comes from East Berks Boat Company, the original source of the device, which was located on Wargrave Road, Henly on Thames, England. It was developed by John Weatherlake. It originated sometime in the 1960s and was made by the Henley Plastics

Company. For a long period the Ebbco was the most popular plastic sextant in Europe, but not as well known in the US. This company discontinued business in July, 1990, after which the model was distributed by Plastimo in France under the name of "Antares." It seems the market for these was kept active by a maritime regulation in France that required a sextant and tables to be onboard every recreational vessel going offshore (though knowledge of celestial was not required). That requirement was dropped in Jan, 2005, and after that the Ebbcos were no longer in the Plastimo catalog and have not been available. The Henley Plastics company had restructured twice in different locations during this period, but they seem to have discontinued business at about that time.

The patent number on all Ebbco units turns out to be the application number. The actual patent seems not to have been filed. There is hearsay indication that the original mold was destroyed in a fire, but we do not have proof of this.

4. Davis history

The Davis sextants originated in 1963 with a Mark 2 model, essentially the same as the later Mark 3, except the earlier had an allen key adjustment for the index mirror. The instrument appears to be modeled after the US Navy life boat sextant made by the Culver Co in Chicago from 1940 to about 1953. A Mark 12 followed in about 1966, which had a knob to move the Index arm, but the dial was still of the Mark 3 type. Shortly after than the Mark 15 was introduced which had a micrometer drum . The Mark 25 originated in 1980, which was a milestone in sextant technology as it was the first to offer a full-view mirror, a technology that Davis Instruments developed and patented.

The sextants and their parent company are named after their developer, William A. Davis, originally from England, who started the company in San Leandro, CA. The company has been located in Hayward, CA not far from the original location, under the present management since 1987.

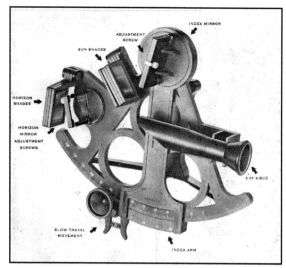

Figure A-3. *The original Davis Mark 12 from about 1966 or so. It was the forerunner of the Mark 15 and Mark 25. It was a vernier sextant with a knob to assist in fine adjustments. There was no telescope.*

The original manuals for the Mark 2 and Mark 12 were written by William A. Davis and called *How to Find Your Position with a Sextant,* dated 1966. A second edition came out in 1968 with a co-author Stephen M. Russell under the title *How to Find Your Position with the Master Sextant,* which is possibly the date of the first Mark 15, although they used this model name for the Mark 12 as well. The Mark 15 was already an established product when the current management took over in 1969.

5. Mirror as artificial horizon

At one point our best artificial horizon was a large, quality plate-glass mirror sitting on top of a high bird feeder in an open back yard. It was leveled with a precision machinist's level and shimmed with business cards for final adjustment. With such a rig, you have a large view of the sky and can walk around it for different bearings. It is difficult to do stars from a liquid surface, but this does the job. It takes some effort to get it level, but even if off a bit this is a good way to get started on artificial horizons.

You will know from your results when you get it right, and can even develop a table of corrections for various bearings. Ways to improvise become clear as you get underway on such a project.

6. Full-view mirror properties

The full-view horizon mirrors developed by Davis are described in their patent as: "It transmits light in the orange-red range—such being the same range as emanates from the horizon at dusk and dawn when so many star shots are taken. It reflects light in the blue-green-yellow range; such range includes the dominant wavelengths of light emitted from most celestial objects. It also transmits light in the violet-blue range, as shown in Figure A-4. Therefore, the spectrally selective beamsplitter, used in this unusual manner involving transmission from one side and reflection from the other, can be of great advantage, especially for dawn and dusk use."

7. Method 1 background

The numerical solutions to what we call Method 1 is in *Bowditch*, Table 16—Distance by Vertical Angle Measured Between Waterline at Object and Top of Object. The solutions are based upon the following simplifying assumptions:

(1) the eye of the observer is at sea level

(2) the sea surface between the observer and the object is flat,

(3) atmospheric refraction is negligible, and

(4) the waterline at the object is vertically below the peak of the object.

According to *Bowditch*, the error due to the height of eye of the observer does not exceed 3 percent of the distance-off for sextant angles less than 20° and heights of eye less than one-third of the object height. The error due to the waterline not being below the peak of the object does not exceed 3 percent of the distance-off when the height of eye is less than one-third of the object height and the offset of the waterline from the base of the object is less than one-tenth of the distance-off. Errors due to earth's curvature and

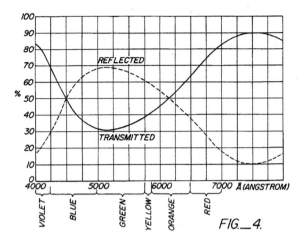

Figure A-4. *Davis beam-converger "full-view mirror" properties, from 1983 US Patent No. 4,421,407.*

atmospheric refraction are negligible for cases of practical interest.

Our approximate solution (which includes the same qualifiers *Bowditch* outlines for the correct solution) is derived as follows, using D = distance to base of target in nmi, H = height of object above water level in ft, and angular height of top to waterline = α in degrees:

The exact result is $D = H/\tan(\alpha)$, but when α is a small angle (less than 15°), we can approximate $\tan(\alpha)$ by $\alpha \times \pi/180$. Thus we get

$D = H/(\alpha \times \pi/180)$, and then convert to feet by multiplying by (1 nmi/6076 ft) to get

$$D = H/\alpha/106,$$

which we approximate further to get

$$D = H/100/\alpha$$

for the sake of ease in memory. In our example from Figure 3-1, H = 240 ft and $\alpha = 2°$, we get 1.2 nmi with the approximation, whereas the exact answer is 1.13, which is 6% lower. To fine tune the approximation, just add 6% to your answer.

Testimonials

[1] "I used *Starduster's* elegant Japanese made sextant while a shipmate backed me up with my old plastic Ebbco. Significantly, there was rarely any major difference in our selected altitudes." This is from an interesting account of the 1976 Vic-Maui Yacht Race by skipper/navigator William Francis. See www.vicmaui.org/pdfs/vic-maui_by_sextant.pdf.

[2] Trevor Robertson, recipient of the 2009 Blue Water Metal from Cruising Club of America (shared with Annie Hill), did an 8,000 mile, cruise in a 34-foot wooden sloop from Western Australia to South Africa "navigating only by plastic sextant and lead line." See www.cruising-club.org/awards/awards_bluewater_2009.htm

[3] Hewitt Schlereth, author of the *Commonsense Navigation* series, among many other books, gave this report from his 2009 cel nav course. Sights were taken under sail in the British Virgin Islands. The temperature was in the 70s without bright sun.

"What I did at sea was have the guys take turns taking and timing sights while I wrote down the time, altitudes and GPS position for each sight. I've had a fair amount of personal experience with plastic sextants—the only sextant I had for several years was an Ebbco. At the time ('72-'75) the only check available was the DR. Back then, I considered LOPs and fixes within 5-10 percent of the distance run between DRs normal.

Now being able to compare the Mark 15 Davis against my GPS (a Garmin 72) I discovered these students were consistently getting LOP intercepts of less than 1.2', Toward or Away, with no systematic trends detected. Indeed two of them routinely got results below 1'. The champ was our shipmate from Switzerland who nailed one at 0.1'. Probably a fluke, but his confidence as well as everybody else's soared.

The IC was checked before and after each sight session using the horizon. The values varied from 1 to 2', off and on the scale, checked before and after each sight session. All students shared

the same Mark 15. Everyone took 4 rounds (1 to 3 sights each) each day for 5 days: morning, noon and afternoon sun sights, and a round of star-planet sights each evening. The experience was certainly a good testimony for the plastic sextants". (*Authors's note: not mentioned was the students obviously had good instruction from Hewitt on the use of a sextant!*)

[4] Peter Hakel posted in the NavList discussion group on August 28, 2010 his recent Davis Mark 15 shot of a Jupiter lunar, in which he obtained a cleared lunar distance equal to the correct lunar distance within 0.1'. He pointed out immediately that this was "Definitely fortuitous, nevertheless pleasant to see." Other experts agreed that there is chance involved, and nuances to the clearing process can alter results sometimes. There have been suggestions over the years in this forum that 1 to 3 arc minutes might be more typical on the cleared distance errors on individual sights with plastic sextants, which we would agree with based on our own results.

Nevertheless, we repeat what we have stated earlier, that when many such sights are taken and averaged, we can indeed get a useful emergency longitude, and in any event productively investigate this fascinating process with a plastic sextant used carefully. For details of his sights, see http://www.fer3.com/arc, which is also an excellent resource for all matters celestial.

[5] Steve Miller of Chapman School of Seamanship provided this recent set of plastic and metal sextant altitude measurements made offshore of Stuart, FL, underway at about 7 kts.

Using a Mark 15, three solar IC measurements with a Baader filter yielded an average IC = 0.7' On ±1.0' (spread in values), with the determined SD = 15.4 ± 0.4'. True SD was 15.8, which shows that although the measurements from varied by 1', they were consistent in getting about the right SD in each case. Four sights from 0958 to 1136 EDT yielded intercepts relative to true GPS at each sight of 6.3 A 093, 4.1 A 095, 2.8 A 098, and 4.6 T 110 for an average of 2.2 A. A very narrow angle running fix from first to last was off by 28 miles, but this is not bad at all for sights that differed in Zn by just 17°. The sextant was in the sun for a long time here, and we do note a systematic change in the intercepts, getting bigger with time. We do not have an IC at the end, which would have pointed out any possible change that might have accounted for this.

Just after these, Steve took a series with a Tamaya Jupiter metal sextant, and obtained three solar IC measurements with average 1.3 Off ±0.1, with the 4 SD measurements yielding 16.1 ±0.1. These sights from 1105 to 1220 EDT yielded: 1.2A 103, 1.7A 105, 1.0A 109, and 0.2A 125, for an average of 1.0'A, again all reduced from the actual GPS positions at the time of each sight. A running fix from first to last was off by 6.6 nmi, which again is not more than we could ask for with an intersection angle of just 22°. All sights are Away, which is a hint of a systematic error in some stage of the process.

So for a cursory comparison in just these few sights we have an average plastic intercept of 2' with a spread of ±5' and a metal average intercept of 1.0' with a spread of ±0.7', a difference in keeping with the values anticipated in the text.

The systematic behavior noted in both sets of sights might be accounted for from the environment. The conditions were squally that day with distant squalls forming and dissipating. This can affect the view to the horizon as the haze layer changes, and this would also affect the plastic data differently from the metal data because they have such different telescopes.

The plastic sights could perhaps be improved by a series closer together in time, followed by a second IC check, then slope analyzed.

[6] Plastic-metal lunar comparisons also from Steve Miller provide good typical results. Using a Mark 15 and a Tamaya for measuring lunar distance to Jupiter on 7/29/10. The sights were alternated, which somehow introduced a systematic behavior of the plastic data. The second sight of each set returning to the plastic was higher. Except for two that were clearly off, these are good examples of "typical" sight sessions.

Steve has many examples of better lunars, both metal and plastic. The average of several sight sessions will always improve the final results. A plot of the theoretical slope is usually helpful in the analysis.

Results are shown below compared to the computed values. Plots of the individual sights are shown in Figure A-5. The calculated slopes are only 28.4'/60m, showing this is not an optimum body to use at this time. Slopes some 20% steeper are possible.

Solar IC, SD true = 15.8				
On	60-	Off	IC	SD
31.8	33.2	26.8	-2.5	14.7
29.0	36.7	23.3	-2.9	13.1
31.5	35.1	24.9	-3.3	14.1
	MK 15	Avg=	-2.9	13.9
28.1	29.9	30.1	1.0	14.6
28.3	29.7	30.3	1.0	14.7
28.4	30.0	30.0	0.8	14.6
	Tamaya	Avg=	0.9	14.6

Mark 15			Tamaya		
Time minutes	LD error	Lon error	Time minutes	LD error	Lon error
44.17	-1.8'	54'	41.23	1.1	32'
45.50	0.4'	-12'	47.75	1.9	56'
49.85	-5.6'		48.90	1.3	39'
51.38	-1.8'	54'	52.67	0.4	12'
54.87	-7.9'		53.77	0.7	21'
56.15	-2.4'	72'	57.28	0.7	21'
Avg =	-1.4'	42'	Avg =	1.0'	30'

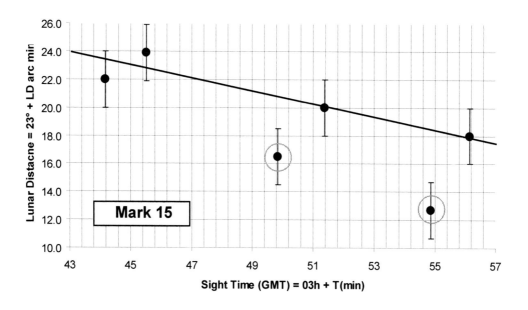

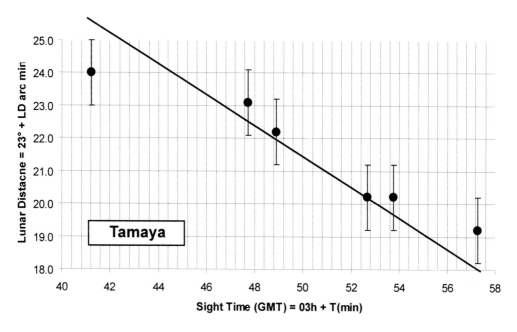

Figure A-5. *Lunar distance sights from Capt. Steve Miller, author of* The Captain's Moon, *which details procedures and analysis of lunar photography, including a unique full set of daily images over a full lunar cycle. In the Mark 15 data, the 3rd and 5th sights were notably off the theoretical slope and could be discarded from the average.*

Glossary

accuracy	The specification of how much a measured value differs from the true value. It is often specified as the uncertainty in a value, such as 100 ± 10. It should not be confused with the precision of the value or its uncertainty. See precision.
alignment	Here used often to mean the final step in a sextant sight when we have the reflected view of the object in the horizon mirror in line with the direct view of the horizon, or another landmark for piloting measurements, in the horizon glass.
altitude	In celestial navigation the same as height. See height.
altitude intercepts	The difference between Ho and Hc in a celestial sight reduction. Also called "a-values."
arc	That part of the circumference of a sextant frame that includes the gear rack and angle labels.
assumed position	An artificial location near your estimated position chosen to facilitate the use of sight reduction tables.
a-value	Same as altitude intercept.
away	Micrometer drum turning direction that decreases the sextant angle. See also toward.
away (A)	Altitude intercept label when Ho is less than Hc.
azimuth (Zn)	The true bearing of a celestial body.
Beam Converger	The name Davis Instruments uses for their full-view mirror on the Mark 25.
calculated altitude (Hc)	The calculated altitude of a celestial body from a given position at a given time. It is often called calculated height, and (presumably) hence its abbreviation. See also height.
calculator	See navigation calculator.
celestial bodies	Usually refers to the bodies visible to the naked eye including sun, moon, stars, Venus, Jupiter, Mars, and Saturn. Mercury can indeed be seen, but only rarely and only low in the sky, and is thus not usually considered in this group.
celestial navigation	The process of using the angular heights of celestial bodies above the horizon at known times to find your latitude and longitude on earth. The normal process requires a sextant, a watch, a Nautical Almanac, and sight reduction tables.

circle of position (COP)	A circle, or sector of a circle, on the chart that you know you are located on, but you do not know where you are on that circle. It is a "circular line of position." They are obtained by determining your distance from the landmark located at the center of the circle by some piloting technique. See also line of position.
clearing	The process of making all needed corrections to a lunar distance measurement in preparation for finding the correct time or a longitude.
collimation tube	Same as sight tube.
declination (dec)	A term used in celestial navigation. It is equivalent to the latitude of the celestial body. It is listed in the Nautical Almanac. See also Greenwich hour angle.
depth contour	A line on the chart marking equal depths.
dip	Used to refer to how much the apparent horizon differs from the true horizon, expressed in arc minutes. It depends on the height of eye.
dip short	Method of correcting sextant sights when using a shoreline for the horizon that is closer to you than the true sea horizon.
elevation	See height.
frame	The base plate of a sextant, usually in the pie shape of an arc sector spanning just over one-sixth of a circle in keeping with the name "sextant."
full-view mirror	A horizon mirror with special coating that allows light to be both reflected and transmitted from the same surface. They are also called full-horizon, or whole-horizon mirrors. These mirrors when used replace the traditional horizon mirror and horizon glass with this one special coated glass.
gear slack	Used here to mean we can get different readings on the sextant depending on which way we make the final turn of the micrometer drum during alignment. Plastic sextants require special procedures to minimize this effect, although in principle it can be present in any instrument.
GMT	See universal time.
Google Earth	A free software program that can be used to view the geography, terrain, and structures on the earth and its oceans with remarkable detail in many cases. It requires an Internet connection.
Greenwich hour angle (GHA)	A term used in celestial navigation. It is equivalent to the longitude of the celestial body. It is listed in the Nautical Almanac. See also declination.
height	The elevation of a landmark, referenced to mean sea level on maps and to mean high water on US nautical charts.

height (Hs, Ho, Hc)	Often used to refer to the angular height of a celestial body above the horizon, and in this use is identical to altitude. See calculated altitude, sextant altitude, and observed altitude.
height of eye (HE)	The height of an observer's eye above the water level.
horizon glass	The empty space or plain glass next to the horizon mirror, through which we view the horizon or a land mark for sextant sights.
horizon mirror	The second mirror that incident light rays strike producing the reflected image used for alignment with the direct view of the horizon seen through the horizon glass, which is next to it. The horizon mirror and horizon glass are located in line with the telescope and they do not move during a sight.
horizontal sextant angles	Angles measured with a sextant held horizontally, frame parallel to the horizon. Horizontal angles are in principle equivalent to taking two compass bearings and subtracting them, although the results are extremely more accurate with a sextant.
index correction (IC)	The correction made for an index error.
index error	An error in the sextant angle that occurs when the index mirror is not perfectly parallel to the horizon mirror with the index arm set to 0°0'. It is usually treated more as a measurable "offset" than an actual "error" in the sight process. The numerical correction for this is called index correction (IC), which is numerically identical. See also side error.
index mirror	The first mirror that incident light rays strike on their way to producing the reflected image in the horizon mirror. It is located at the top of the index arm, at its pivot point. The index mirror rotates when the index arm is moved to different sextant angles.
inverting the sextant	A procedure used to take star sights when pre-computation was not done. It consists of turning the sextant (set to 0° 0') upside down and pointing it to a star that is viewed in the direct view, and then moving the index arm to bring the horizon up to the star. Then the sextant is returned to normal orientation to complete the sight.
leave	Our term for the moment when the direct view and reflected view of the horizon or a star first appears to be no longer in alignment as we turn the micrometer drum slowly in the direction from which we approached the alignment. The point when the alignment was first made, we call the touch point.
line of position (LOP)	A line on the chart that you know you are located on, but you do not know exactly where you are on that line. See also circle of position.
local hour angle (LHA)	A term used in celestial navigation. It is the equivalent to the longitude of a celestial body relative to the observer's meridian. The longitude of a celestial body relative to the Greenwich meridian is called the Greenwich hour angle.

lunar	The name given to the process of finding correct time and longitude by measuring the lunar distance.
lunar distance (LD)	The diagonal arc distance between an edge of the moon and a neighboring celestial body along its path through the Zodiac.
Mark 15	A model of the Davis plastic sextant. It is black plastic, with a traditional split mirror and 3x27 telescope.
Mark 25	A model of the Davis plastic sextant, which is same as the Mark 15, but in gray plastic, with full-view mirror and a lighted dial. It is reported by the manufacturer that the Mark 25 uses "an upgraded plastic that is very stable."
Mark 3	The simplest of the plastic sextants from Davis. It is a vernier sextant without micrometer drum and without telescope.
meridian	A line of longitude. See also parallel.
micrometer drum	The knob marked in arc minutes attached to the worm gear at the base of the index arm. They often include a vernier scale for estimating the tenths of an arc minute, or sometimes seconds of arc.
Nautical Almanac	The yearly publication of astronomical positions of the celestial bodies and related tables used for celestial navigation produced by the United States Naval Observatory in collaboration with its British counterparts.
navigation calculator	A computer program in a handheld calculator that can compute almanac data and do sight reductions. There are also numerous software programs for a PC that do this, as well as online resources. There are similar programs for computing sextant piloting results from vertical and horizontal sextant angles. Computed solutions for both celestial and piloting are typically more accurate than the corresponding tabular results, and usually more convenient.
observed altitude (Ho)	The observed altitude in a celestial sight reduction. It is Hs corrected for IC, dip, refraction, semidiameter, and parallax. See height.
off the scale	A sextant reading that is below 0° 0', which puts the index mark to the right of 0° 0'. The result is effectively a negative number, so the actual angle that it is "off the scale" must be found by subtracting the sextant reading from 0° 0'. A measurement that is off the scale means the object you are looking at in the reflected view is lower than the reference being used in the direct view.
on the scale	A normal sextant reading, with the index to the left of 0° 0', so it is a positive value. The object you are seeing in the reflected view is above the reference you are using in the direct view. See off the scale.
parallel	A line of latitude. See also meridian.
piloting	The process of finding out where you are relative to charted landmarks.

precision	The numerical detail to which a numerical value is specified. The number 10 is less precise than 10.3, which in turn is less precise than 10.38. Precision should not be confused with accuracy, which is an entirely different concept, although there are reasonable expectations for consistent usage between them. (In this text we push the envelope somewhat when we state results of a series of plastic sextant measurements such as "a = 2.3 ± 5 (spread in values)." This is shorthand notation for what should be a more careful statistical description of the multiple measurements and how they varied.)
pre-computation	The process of predicting the height and bearing of a body before taking the sight. It is standard procedure for star sights, and useful for some moon sights. It can be productively applied to lunar distance sights as well.
range	The distance to a landmark from the observer.
range	The alignment of any two landmarks on the horizon. When the marks are specifically put there (by the USCG for example) for navigation it is called a navigational range, otherwise it is called a natural range. Also called transit.
refraction	The bending of light rays as they enter the earth's atmosphere from outer space. The amount of bend is maximum for bodies on the horizon (about 34.5' at Hs=0°) and then decreases rapidly with altitude (10' at 5°, then 5' at 10°, and 0.1' at 15°) in normal temperature and pressure.
rolling	A boat motion in a seaway that is a rotation about an axis along the centerline of the boat. See also yawing.
semidiameter (SD)	Half the diameter of the sun or moon. It is called semidiameter instead of radius because refraction flattens the visible disk of these bodies into an ellipse, and this dimension of an ellipse is called a semidiameter.
set and wait	Our name for the process of presetting the sextant to a view that is just short of actual alignment, and then waiting for the alignment to occur on its own as the body rises or sets, at which time we record the time of alignment without further sextant adjustments.
sextant altitude (Hs)	The sextant angle read directly from the sextant. Sometimes called sextant height or sextant altitude. See height.
side error	A sextant error that occurs when either the index mirror or horizon mirror is not perpendicular to the frame of the sextant. If offsets the reflected image to the side of the direct image in the horizon mirror. See also index error.
sight	The process of measuring the sextant height of a celestial body, or the angle between two landmarks using a sextant.

sight reduction	The name given to the process of converting celestial (altitude) sights to a position on the chart. Sight reduction can be done by computation or by tables. Popular tables for the process are called Pub. 249 and Pub. 229. There are also sight reduction tables in the Nautical Almanac, usually called the NAO Tables. The roughly analogous process applied to lunar sights is called clearing.
sight tube	An empty cylinder about an inch in diameter often with an empty eyepiece at one end used in place of a sextant telescope for some applications in sextant piloting. It has no lenses or magnification and is used only to guide the view toward the index glass. Also called a collimation tube.
slope method	Our name for the process of evaluating celestial sights taken over a short time period with the corresponding theoretical computations of these same values. Though the data might not agree point for point, the slope (rate of change with time) of the measured values can be evaluated relative to the correct slope.
solar IC method	Our name for using the upper and lower limbs of the sun or moon for index correction measurement.
split mirror	A name often used for the traditional horizon mirror that is half mirror and half open or plain glass. The other option for the horizon mirror is called a full-view mirror.
station pointer	Same as three-arm protractor.
three-arm protractor	A plotting tool with three arms that can be used to find the unique observation point from which three charted landmarks would appear to have the angular separations you observed with a sextant. Also called a station pointer.
three-point fix	The process of finding your location by measuring the sextant angles between three landmarks on the horizon. Also called "the three-body" fix.
touch	Our term for the moment when the direct view and reflected view of the horizon or a star first appears in alignment as we turn the micrometer drum slowly in one direction only. When the apparent alignment breaks as we continue in the same direction we call it the leave point.
toward	Micrometer drum turning direction that increases the sextant angle. See also away.
toward (T)	Altitude intercept label when Ho is greater than Hc.
transit	Same as range.
universal time (UT)	The international time standard used in navigation. It was once called Greenwich Mean Time (GMT). It is sometimes called universal coordinated time (UTC).
vernier scale	An ingenious scheme of scale placements that allow intermediate values to be determined.

vertical sextant angles	Angles measured with a sextant held in the vertical (normal) position, frame perpendicular to the horizon. See also horizontal angles.
watch error (WE)	The difference between watch time and the correct time in the time zone the watch is set to. If the watch is set to PDT (ZD=+7) and the correct time is 13:45:40 PDT and the watch reads 13:45:35, then the WE = 5s Slow. Then UT = 13:45:35 + 07:00:00 + 00:00:05 = 20:45:40.
watch time (WT)	The actual time read from the navigator's watch at the time of a sight. This time must be converted to universal time before the sight reduction can be carried out. Universal time = watch time ± watch error ± zone description.
whole-horizon mirror	Same as full-view mirror.
worm gear	The conical gear attached to the index arm that engages the index arm with the gear teeth on the arc of the sextant. It is disengaged to move the arm to larger angles, or moved along the arc by turning micrometer drum.
yawing	A boat motion in a seaway that is a rotation about an axis perpendicular to the deck, located somewhere near the middle of the boat. See also rolling.
Zodiac	The broad line of constellations in the stellar sky though which the sun, moon, and planets travel throughout the year.
zone description (ZD)	The zone description of the watch being used for watch time is the number of hours between watch time (corrected for watch error) and universal time. ZD is + if you add hours to WT to get UT, and negative otherwise.

About the Author

David Burch is a recipient of the Institute of Navigation's Superior Achievement Award for outstanding performance as a practicing navigator. He has logged more than 70,000 miles at sea including twelve transoceanic yacht races, with several first place victories and a passage record for boats under 36 feet that lasted 16 years. He also navigated the only American entry in the storm-ridden 1993 Sydney to Hobart Race. On the academic side, he is a past Fulbright Scholar with a PhD in Physics.

As the Founding Director of Starpath School of Navigation in Seattle and one of its lead instructors, he has developed teaching materials and taught navigation and marine weather for more than 20 years. He continues to work on the development of online courses in marine weather and navigation at starpath.com. He is a contributing editor of Blue Water Sailing Magazine.

Other books by David Burch

Radar for Mariners

Emergency Navigation

The Star Finder Book

Fundamentals of Kayak Navigation

Celestial Navigation

Inland and Coastal Navigation

Modern Marine Weather

The Barometer Handbook

and these student Study Guides

Radar Workbook (with Larry Brandt)

Weather Workbook

Onboard Exercise Book

Navigation Workbook

CPSIA information can be obtained at www.ICGtesting.com
Printed in the USA
LVOW052130170512

282259LV00004B/93/P